Good and Miserable

Why many "good" people are also very unhappy.

by Neil Schulenburg

Isbn-13: 978-1543017366

Isbn-10: 1543017363

www.neilschulenburg.com

Acknowledgements

There are many people who have contributed to this work. A special thank you goes to the clients that have shared so much of their personal experiences. Their willingness to be open in order to help others is a great blessing.

A number of people have helped by providing encouragement and by dedicating personal time to the difficult task of editing. Kathryn Schulenburg, Alison Cox, Debby Temmer, Kailey Temmer, Lori Nichols and several others from the Centered for Life counseling center played a major role.

Without all of these people and their gracious contribution, the publication of this book would not be possible.

Foreword

We, in the United States and other western nations, live in a very rich and productive society. In many ways, we are the most blessed people in the world. At the same time, our highly-developed culture has given rise to unique problems. We have a divorce rate that exceeds 50%. Many have attained a very high standard of living but have little job satisfaction. Stress is affecting us in epidemic proportions. Most of us are able to own a motor vehicle, many have more than one. At the same time, road rage seems to be more common than ever before. We have more possessions than most societies but we have little real satisfaction in life. Addictions seem to claim far too many of us. What is it about our society that leads us to such self-destruction? We seem to have so much, but have very little peace and contentment.

It is amazing to see how many of us live our lives year after year in a kind of self-delusion. We think that we are doing our best in life only to come to a sudden and terrible realization that we are in fact utterly miserable. The situation is something of a puzzle to us because we believe that we have done our best, only to find out that the outcome is not as we expected. Our misery seems to be manifest in the very areas of life that we cherish most. If we have emphasized doing our best in the areas of career or family, ironically those same objects of our devotion crumble in spite of all our efforts.

This may sound like an overly negative point of view but this is indeed where many of us find ourselves. We try very hard to protect the most sacred areas of our lives. In doing so, our grasp tightens on them resulting in death by smothering. What is more ironic is that the damage is not limited only to the objects of our devotion. Usually we are casualties as well.

If you count yourself among the people who are suffering in this way, don't despair. There is hope. This book is dedicated to providing help. The first step is to gain an understanding about the "try hard / self-destruct" existence and its origins. With a little insight into the nature of our souls, new resolution can be found to open the door for inner change.

You may not think that this book is for you. The difficulty is that those of us who try hard in life rarely admit that anything is wrong until there is a major crisis. Our job is to hold it all together. An admission that there is a problem would burst our bubble of self-made security. Before you run off to slay another dragon, take a quick look at the list of symptoms at the end of Chapter One. If anything on that list looks vaguely familiar, I encourage you to slow down and read this book more carefully. It may be the most important thing that you will ever do for yourself and for your loved ones.

Do you feel like there's something wrong but you're not sure exactly what it is? Are you always doing your best, but not experiencing joy in your life?

Good and Miserable

Contents

Chapter 1
Introduction

Jackie is a good worker and has always tried hard in every area of her life. She was a great student in school and today she is the "go to" person at her job. Her conduct is highly respected both professionally and personally. She is a leader in her church. It seems like she has it all together. What others don't know is that Jackie is not happy with her life. Her moods swing to periods of depression. She can't enter into close relationships with people. When others try to get close to her she has to look for a logical reason for their interest. It is hard for her to accept others in their weakness and it is threatening to her to be around those who are strong. She is much better at staying busy in life rather than with living it.

Jackie is a person with a performance priority. She is one of the walking wounded. She may appear to have everything going for her, but inside she is bound by a host of negative emotions. She may exist in this state for a considerable time. If she is fortunate, somewhere along the line the train will jump the tracks. She will become so dissatisfied with her life that she will search for help. The dissatisfaction might be with broken or non-existent relationships, the downturns in her mood or simply a lack of joy in life.

There is good and bad news associated with this condition. The bad news is that quite a number of us are afflicted. What makes the bad new worse is that most of the afflicted don't know it. The good news is that this condition does not have to be permanent. There are things that we can do to obtain inner healing and achieve change.

Good People

Do you think of yourself as a good person? As a rule, are you better than others? Most of us would respond to a question like that with an immediate, "Of course not!" Think about the question honestly. Most of us will think in terms of how we should answer. The correct response is that we have all been created equal and that God shows no partiality to men and woman. What we are looking for in this discussion is not the correct response. What we are driving toward, and what we all want to know is the truth about who we really are. What makes us behave the way that we do? Really dig into your personal feelings about who you are and respond again. Do you like to think of yourself as a good person, one who is better than most other people?

You may not feel that your value is greater than others, but what about how you conduct yourself in this world. People with a performance priority like to think of themselves as people who are able to do things better than others. At the same time in their hearts they feel a low sense of self-worth. They are only comfortable when they can demonstrate to themselves and to others that they can perform better than the rest. Are you the kind of person who gives most things your best effort? If you cannot do well in an activity do you shy away? Are you the one that is considerate of others? How do you feel about those who are inconsiderate? Do they really set you off?

Many of us have spent our lives maximizing our personal performance in every area in order to be successful. The drive for success has a number of motivational components. The most basic is simple survival. Another is the desire to receive affirmation as a worthwhile individual. Perhaps the most powerful is the desire for affection and acceptance from others.

The drive to be successful in these areas is a part of being human and does not necessarily result in dysfunctional behavior or emotional pain. Unfortunately for a number of us, this drive can dominate our basic way of thinking. The domination of one set of inner beliefs is what some psychotherapists call a priority. The drive for emotional survival based upon personal performance is what we will call a performance priority. It will be shown that this inner belief system is the root of much of our misery.

This book is not about the person with an obsession about perfection. Various anxiety disorders and personality disorders can present in this way but it is not the same problem as a performance priority. It isn't about performing to be the center of attention. Dysfunctional family systems and still other personality disorders can be indicated in this situation. Neither is it about the person who must be in control at all times. This behavior can be the result of early shaming or family of origin chaos. What will be addressed here is a more subtle, insidious and devastating problem. The performance priority is insidious because it is by nature deceptive. What can be more destructive than doing harm to ourselves when we think that we are doing or being good?

Simply stated, *the performance priority is an inner belief system that emphasizes personal achievement to earn one's position of worth and emotional safety.*

Miserable People

You might be wondering, "What is really so bad with trying to be good?" The answer is really quite simple. People with this condition are so focused on their own performance that every aspect of life becomes soured. You may be thinking that this doesn't sound like you. Remember that this is by nature a deceptive condition. Much of what influences us occurs at a level that is outside of our conscious awareness. To see if you might be a person who is influenced by a performance priority, check the symptoms that apply to you. Remember, if you are influenced by this condition denial is likely to be strong because being "ok" is so important. Try to be honest as you review the list.

The following is a list of symptoms and characteristics that are associated with this syndrome:

Overachieving
People pleasing (happy when you can, unhappy when you can't)
Periods of depression
Difficulty making decisions
Sensitivity to criticism
Feelings of unworthiness (masked by a veneer of competence)
Fear of failure privately (a public achiever)

High level of stress and anxiety

Anger and bitterness

Jealousy and envy

Aversion to inconsiderate behavior in others

Aversion to neediness in others

Aversion to irresponsibility in others

Difficulty entering intimate relationships

Difficulty showing and receiving love freely

Difficulty forgiving and receiving forgiveness.

If you checked four or more of these items, learning more about the nature of a performance priority might open the door to new freedom and emotional health.

This may feel like the theme of your life.

Chapter 2
Where It All Starts

It is probably best to begin with an overview of how the human personality is formed. It is the position of this writer that there are a number of influencing factors. Biology plays a part in that human beings are predisposed in certain ways according to their genetic makeup. Some are more sensitive than others. Their nervous systems are more responsive to stimuli from the environment. Some are more energetic or athletic. Experience plays a part in our personality formation in that we learn from life as we develop. Patterns of thinking and behavior are assimilated as they are discovered to be useful for our survival. Emotional memories have a far-reaching impact on our future behavior. Another area that influences who we are is our spiritual condition. Initially, God equips us with a certain temperament. Many believe that we are given a predisposing spirit before we are born.

The area of personality development that is influential in the origins of the performance priority is the area of learning. As we develop, experiences occur that prove to be positive or negative regarding our personal survival. We assimilate and carry forward those things that we think and feel will be useful. Those things that do not contribute are discarded. What develops is what some theorists call a lifestyle. Lifestyle in this sense is not concerned with clothing, houses or cars. This term is used to describe the person's approach to succeeding in life. It is a set of filters and thought patterns by which all things are judged and all behavioral responses are generated.

Most human development theorists maintain that the majority of the human personality is formed by age eight. Certainly, additional influences take place after that point, but most of the pattern is in place by that time. It is for that reason that therapists explore early life experiences like family of origin conditions to gain clues to a person's current emotional state.

People with a performance priority learn that their worth in life is based upon what they do. The message can be loud and clear as with the domineering parent who loads a child with family responsibilities. This child learns quickly that his or her worth is based upon their utility to the family. The origins of the problem can also be very subtle. Some parents are emotionally unavailable to their children. The child might learn that some attention can be gained by being good or achieving in school or sports. A similar situation that contributes to this condition is when the parent selectively rewards responsible behavior with attention or affection. Perhaps they repeat a message that being constructive, making good grades or being the good child is the only thing that pleases them.

It may seem rather harmless to give a child responsibility in the family or to reward responsible behavior. Effective parents must teach these things to their children. The problem arises when the child is valued only for his or her responsible behavior. They are only loved when they are good. The concept of giving and receiving love freely, not for what they do but for who they are, is lost. The concept of grace in relationship must be taught as a balance to lessons about responsibility.

The picture of someone who continually tries to be good but knows that they can never be good enough begins to take shape. It spills over into all of their relationships including their relationship with God. These people typically try to be good Christians by obeying the word of God, by yielding their will in every way they can think of, by memorizing scriptures or paying tithes. Difficulty occurs when they have done the things that they feel are their part of the bargain and God doesn't deliver what they expect in return. In their hearts, they know that they could never do enough to measure up, so they feel undeserving of His favor. When they do something that they feel is appropriate to earn favor and don't receive the expected benefit, the response can be anger or depression.

Most people will read the description above and immediately identify the fact that these people are living counter to the message of grace. The performance priority, as we will see, is actually the antithesis of the Christian concept of grace. We have been taught what grace is all about. Most of us have a level of intellectual understanding concerning the concept of grace as unmerited favor. That doesn't mean that we have assimilated that truth in our lives. We can have a good grasp of a concept intellectually and at the same time have none of it in our hearts. Some have said that the 12" from our heads to our hearts is the longest trip in the world. Remember that we are looking at psychological phenomena. A performance priority is a deeply rooted pattern of thinking that may be out of the reach of our conscious thought processes.

In my own practice a number of people have been identified with this syndrome. In most cases the persons affected have had comprehensive Christian training. They are well versed on the meaning of grace. Some are in positions of leadership in large Christian organizations. Christians, even the ones that we look up to, are not immune to illness in this world. They just have a better answer to the problem. Are all Christians experiencing victory in every area of their lives? Are all Christians full of joy and peace?   I think that it is safe to say that they are not. Is it all attributable to sin or is it possible that some of us are incomplete in some way deep in our souls? We must be honest about our experience and be willing to do what is necessary to obtain emotional healing and growth.

God's will is for us to be whole. It is in emotional wholeness that we are able to be all that He has intended for us to be in this world. We are all called to some form of ministry. When emotional clutter is cleared away we become much more effective in our calling for Christ.

It is also God's will for us to be in healthy relationships. We need to be able to be in relationship to fully experience what is intended for all Christians. Christianity is more than a philosophy or a set of guidelines for life. Christianity is about relationship with the Living God. By His Holy Spirit He conforms us to His image to bring about inner healing and to prepare us for the work of service to Him.

As we will see, the Lord is faithful to bring about this healing as we make ourselves available to Him. He is the Wonderful Counselor. As this amazing process unfolds, we become new from the inside out. We discover the joy of a closer relationship to God, the gift of closer relationships with others and freedom from self-torment.

Chapter 3
Case Examples

This section contains four case examples of persons who struggle with a performance priority. These descriptions have been included in order to provide a better understanding of this condition for the reader. The names of the characters have been changed and some details have been modified in order to provide confidentiality for those who have unselfishly agreed to share their stories.

Janet

Janet came to counseling for help with a persistent problem that had followed her throughout the course of her life. She said that there were actually a number of things bothering her. Something deep inside her led her to feel that they were all somehow related to one root issue. She was hoping that counseling could shed some light on the matter.

It was difficult to see how Janet could really have any problems at all. She was an attractive and intelligent young woman with a winning personality. She had a responsible leadership position with a major Christian organization. She came from a Christian family and had been a Christian herself since her youth. At the time of counseling she was finishing her graduate education. All outward appearances indicated that she had what most of us would consider to be the perfect life.

As counseling proceeded she told a different story. Janet sat in nervous anticipation. She wanted to find a solution to her problem and she wanted it sooner rather than later. She was a results oriented person, but had enough sensitivity to the needs of others not to push the therapist too hard. Pleasing others was part of her priority system as well. Even at this early stage it was clear that inner conflicts were creating stress in her life.

Janet was in her early thirties. She had one serious relationship a few years earlier that ended painfully. At the time of counseling she was seeing a very promising young man but their relationship was not progressing. Janet couldn't put her finger on the problem. She liked this man very much, but she could not seem to allow herself to get close to him. She described a lack of feeling regarding this relationship and with life in general.

Relationships can be very difficult for those afflicted with a performance priority. These people have assimilated the belief that they must perform in a certain way to earn acceptance, recognition, affection, or a sense of personal worth. What they do as a career or what they do for others earns their position and defines who they are. When someone else comes along wanting a deeper level of intimacy, the afflicted person is not prepared to reciprocate. The response is often an unbelieving coldness. The question they ask goes something like this, "Ok, you say that you love me ... why?" There is a vigilant search for a reason for any show of affection from others. They have always had to earn their personal value in the past through their actions. It is difficult and sometimes impossible to accept affection with no strings?

Janet was showing a cold non-emotional front, but there was more brewing beneath the surface. She felt terribly guilty about not being able to respond. She wondered why she could not return affection freely to this man in the way that he was showing it to her. The impasse was a source of frustration to her raising her stress level. It sometimes gave rise to tearful outbursts at her boyfriend or periods of depression as she withdrew from him.

Janet was somewhat frustrated with her inability to live up to the standards that she had set for herself. Receiving a promotion or getting a good grade in graduate school didn't seem to bring the expected gratification for her. Her internal belief was that she could have done much better. Certainly, there was someone else who was more deserving than she was. For Janet, most of life had lost its luster.

She would get angry with others, especially if they showed irresponsibility regarding life skills. Since she had adopted the philosophy that competence is paramount in life, she expected others to act as if they felt the same way. When co-workers or friends did not expend the same amount of effort that she did, she would lose patience with them.

When associates disclosed any form of personal neediness she would be repelled. She was not able to show what she thought should be the appropriate empathetic Christian response. Instead there was an immediate aversion to people who were openly in need of her support or attention. This led to breakdowns in personal relationships and further feelings of guilt and loneliness.

She would get jealous of her friend's personal and professional successes rather than being able to enter into their joy. Janet's internal belief was that she should be receiving the happiness that these others had. Since she had done all the things that she had known to do and had not received the anticipated reward, something had gone terribly wrong. This was another downward spiral for her. She knew that jealousy was an inappropriate response, but she couldn't change it. She felt badly about being jealous. That resulted in more stress and depression.

Decisions were difficult for her. She always struggled harder than others in order to be sure to reach the best outcome no matter what the issue was. The internal belief was that choosing the wrong alternative diminished her personal worth. The best outcome was always of the utmost importance. If something less resulted, there would be a feeling of guilt and personal degradation. In this way of thinking the wrong choice is a terrible thing, whether the matter at hand is choosing a mate or a pair of new shoes.

Janet felt assured that she was a Christian because of all that she had done since her youth, but she had great difficulty accepting God's grace and forgiveness. She felt anxious much of the time and wondered why she did not have the peace that Christians are supposed to enjoy. As a matter of fact, she didn't feel adequate as a Christian at all. She had been in a high-level position in a major Christian organization but never felt that she deserved to be there. There was always a feeling that some other Christian with a much more advanced level of maturity should be in her position.

Her approach to her relationship with Christ was fairly straightforward. She would search her heart as conscientiously as she could. When she discovered something that might be a little too important to her she would immediately yield it to Him. As a matter of fact, being certain that she was yielded was a repeating theme in her descriptions of her Christian experience. Her expectation was that if she was diligent enough to yield all things to Christ, then she should receive all that she needed or wanted from Him. When she had gone through that exercise and her desires were not met, she began to question and get angry with God.

Her anger led her to believe that perhaps God was not good after all. If she had done all that she was required to do and the outcome was still not favorable, perhaps He is not faithful and is not a good God.

Janet would go for periods of time busying herself with career or school and would seem to have some positive momentum. Then her mood would shift and she would find herself in a state of depression. After a time, she would find a way to involve herself in life pursuits again and her mood would lift.

What Janet was describing is what some call the "try hard / give up cycle." Jeff VanVonderen in his book entitled Tired of Trying to Measure Up (1989) describes this painful repeating cycle. His work focuses on how this can develop in those who have been through abusive and shaming experiences. The principle is the same for the one who suffers from a performance priority. Early in life the message is received that survival (physical or emotional) is dependent upon personal performance. There is a focus on self-effort to earn a place in life. As long as there is an outlet for performance the one who is afflicted will busy themselves and be reasonably happy in their activity. When there is a problem or the activity does not produce the desired result, there is a potential to give up. The result is a downward spiral in mood.

When thinking about this situation two pictures come to mind. The first is that of a pet rat running in an exercise wheel.

As long as it can run, it appears to be satisfied. The running doesn't lead anywhere, but the rat stays busy and looks happy. When there is an activity that can provide a means of earning one's position, the afflicted person appears to be in their element. Another image is that of Seligman's dogs (1974). Seligman's research was with dogs that were placed in pens where an electrical shock could be administered. The dogs exhibited what was proposed to be learned helplessness when they received a shock but believed that they had no recourse to escape. They gave up and presented with a depressed state. The same is true for the person with a performance priority when things don't go according to plan. When the activity does not produce the desired result, there is the potential to see no alternative to make things better. The response is to give up in helplessness and hopelessness.

The Beginning for Janet

It was discovered that Janet made every attempt to be a good girl from a very early age. Her mother and father had a conflicted relationship and would fight bitterly. Hearing their fights was extremely upsetting and threatening to Janet. Her response was to retreat to her room to listen to her music box for consolation and safety. She would always check with her mom when she got home from school to see what kind of a mood her father was in. When she got that all-important information, she could then plan her behavior accordingly. She learned that emotional survival was dependent upon her ability to behave in an appropriate fashion based upon the prevailing moods of her angry father.

Janet was not abused as a child. She had what she described as a good family and a happy childhood. Unfortunately, most people describe their early life experiences in that way even when they have gone through some form of abuse. Their family of origin experience is the only one that they know, so to them, it is normal. In Janet's case, there was no outwardly abusive treatment. But living under conditions that were precarious and fearful caused her to adopt a set of beliefs that proved to be self-defeating in later life.

As time progressed, her belief system was reinforced. Janet's younger brother had a disabling mental disorder. She compensated by being less of a burden to the family herself. She attempted to make every area of her life as successful and wrinkle-free as possible. She also felt the burden of contributing to the stability of the family by being the mediator and the one who would bring order to every situation. Janet's parents were both professionals who expected a high level of performance academically. She was acquiring a priority in her belief system to depend on her own performance in life.

In later chapters, recovery will be discussed at length. For now, it is important to know that this condition is not terminal. It is a situation that can be remedied by assimilating new ways of thinking and becoming open to inner healing. Janet was not taught the all-important lesson of grace when she was a child. She learned just the opposite. As parents, we are to be God's representatives to our children. They learn about His nature from our example. It is up to parents to introduce children to the concepts of grace and forgiveness. These ideas must be taught both in theory and in practice. Children need to know what these things are and they need to see them demonstrated by the most significant persons in their lives. If children don't experience grace in their family of origin it is likely that they will not understand the concept later in life and will not be able to live freely as an adult.

Pat

Pat came to counseling to get help with her feelings of stress and anxiety. She was an attractive and energetic woman in her mid-thirties. It soon became apparent that she was a little too energetic. She spoke so fast that her words were barely intelligible. She couldn't sit still in her seat for more than a few moments. She was very thin and spoke often of her high activity level and relatively low interest in time wasting activities like eating.

Pat described herself as a good Christian. In her first few breaths she stated three times that she was a tithing Christian. She did a lot of work for her Church as well. She volunteered to lead Bible studies for the young adult group. She went to services several times on Sunday and through the week. She read the Bible, memorized scriptures and prayed regularly.

Pat's family always went to her for the answer to their problems. She was expected to make things right. Relatives would come to stay with her when they were in need and it was assumed that she would always provide for them. Some would come to her for financial support. She would always make a personal sacrifice in order to meet the need. She said that it had always been that way with her family. Her father was a good man but was distant emotionally. Her mother was stretched thin by the needs of their large family and leaned on

Pat to pick up the slack. Pat ended up caring for her brothers and sisters and doing much of the housework. The needs of the family members seemed to trickle down to her even as a child.

At mid-life, Pat could no longer manage all of the demands on her. She had a good job, a husband and a large extended family that she loved, but she felt that life was like a freight train about to run her down. She had lost weight until she was dangerously thin. She had been hospitalized for a life-threatening illness that was probably stress induced. Her marriage was failing. She was having difficulty with some of her management duties at work. Pat was a good person but she was most certainly a miserable one as well.

Pat is another person who got the message early in life that her worth was based upon what she did for others. She was the responsible child early in life and found herself continuing in that role as an adult. All of the people that were significant to her reinforced that idea. She seemed to be at the mercy of everyone around her. She found it difficult to get off the phone with her mother. She would come home after a long day at work and find herself trapped in endless conversations with her, unable to tell her that she had to go. When there was a death in the family her father just assumed that she would be responsible to make all of the necessary arrangements. When her brother wanted to buy a car, it was assumed that she would provide what he needed financially.

Her marriage relationship was suffering because her husband felt like he couldn't keep up with her. She was working hard to make a home for him but somehow, she was unable to relate to his emotional needs. In all of her busyness

Page 27

she had not nurtured their personal relationship. With her high activity and stress level she was never fully present with her husband. The experience of taking time to be with him, listening to his heart and sharing from her own had never taken place. They had become more like roommates than husband and wife.

In her job, she was known as competent and efficient, but some things were not working there as well. She was having difficulty leaving work before eight or ten at night. She felt that she always had to do everything that she could possibly do to make things right. It was difficult for her to delegate to others. It seemed easier to do the job herself to be sure that it was done right. That level of effort was taking its toll on her physically and at home with her marriage. When it was time to do performance reviews for her employees she would put it off as long as possible. She found it almost impossible to provide any form of negative feedback to her people. Some of these problems were finding their way into her performance reviews as well. Receiving criticism regarding her work performance was very painful and was one of the things that convinced her to get help.

This is an example of someone who knew the message of grace, taught in the church, and completely missed the concept in her own life. What she was living was the antithesis of grace. She understood that grace meant unmerited favor, but the concept was for others not for her. Her way of finding her place in this world was to do things for others. When she was doing things for others she was playing a role that worked for her as a child. She had found a meaningful place with that belief system and for a time it brought rewards. In exchange for her performance behavior, her family bestowed affection and conveyed the idea that she was worthwhile. What she was finding out was that her belief system was not working for her as an adult. In spite of all of Pat's best efforts, her health, happiness, marriage and career were failing.

Personal boundaries had never been established. This is a concept that will be covered in more detail later in our discussion of recovery. At this point it is enough to observe that Pat's priority for performing for others never allowed for basic personal protection for herself.

Pamela

Pamela came to counseling with anxiety issues and concerns regarding her inability to establish and maintain relationships. She was a bright and good-looking woman in her late thirties. She had a successful career with a major corporation but was unhappy most of the time.

Pamela's unhappiness and social isolation lead to some self-medication. Her choice of medication was food. As a result, she was overweight. This condition contributed to her low self-image and added fuel to the negative cycle of medicating and then feeling worse later. Although she was attractive, intelligent and had a personable way with others, Pamela avoided social situations. She had attempted to participate in singles groups in the past and had been disappointed by the results. She had been in a pattern of avoidance for several years thinking that the pain of disappointment was not worth the effort. As time passed the avoidance gave rise to an increasingly negative perception regarding the singles groups. Her only social interaction outside of work was with church sponsored bible studies. She was most comfortable in one particular group where she could be in a leadership role, sharing some personal knowledge and expertise. Going to a group just as herself, with no added value from her capabilities, seemed intimidating. When men took an interest in her she would play the traditional passive female role to the extreme. She would make little proactive effort to move the relationship forward. Her thinking was that the man should show positive proof that he is genuinely interested in her before she could make any investment in him. As a result, Pamela had not been successful in relationships to that point in her life.

Her stress level was quite high, leaving her open to bouts of anger. One of her most difficult challenges was driving to and from work without resorting to road-rage at some of the inconsiderate drivers. Interactions with the rest of the world added more stress to Pamela's life since she told herself subtle lies about each event. These lies were not at the highest levels of her thought life. They were not the kind of conscious thoughts that she could hear pass through her mind. These were at a much lower level where her basic beliefs reside. When she was cut off in traffic she would fall victim to a number of these inner traps. Some of the troublesome beliefs were:

- I need to be first. If I am not first it is terrible.
- I have earned the right to be first in line. Others should respect that. If they don't it is awful.
- I am considerate of others. Since that works for me, others should act that way too.

- Inconsiderate drivers are making an attack on my rights and on me as a person.

Pamela's stress level had risen to the extent that some anxiety disorders were evidenced. She was becoming very fearful of flying. When forced into that situation by work assignments she would experience fearful feelings, rapid heartbeat, dizziness, profuse perspiration and rapid breathing. Her problem had become so controlling that she actually dodged some fairly prestigious assignments at work just to avoid flying.

In counseling, Pamela reported that her early development experience at home was normal and generally positive. As therapy progressed it was discovered that, by far, the memories that she carried forward from her youth were negative. Most memories were of losses or emotional separation. Her father was emotionally unavailable. He worked a lot and was not available to anyone in the family. She felt fairly sure that he loved her but was never told. Her mother leaned on her to meet her own needs for connection rather than supplying the nurturing and constant support required for a developing child. What Pamela learned early in life was that by being a good supportive daughter she would acquire some positive attention and affection. Perhaps if she did well enough in school and was helpful enough to her mother then her father might notice her as well. Certainly, there was no room to express feelings of personal disappointment or anger. Those negative feelings would have to be suppressed in order to be a good daughter.

Keeping those feelings suppressed as an adult led to high levels of stress and anxiety along with periodic outbursts of rage. Pamela was a good child and had become a good adult. She could still be good even with her road rage since she was only shouting at her windshield. The problem she faced was that her emphasis on personal "goodness" was keeping her from living a full life. She could not experience the freedom that is intended for all of God's children. Instead she was falling prey to fear and anxiety.

The prognosis for Pamela was good. She was courageous in her dedication to recovery. She was determined to face her personal issues and move forward toward a better life. She was conscientious concerning counseling and she worked diligently completing all of her assignments. Pamela made steady progress becoming much happier with her life. She was also very positive about the prospects of continued growth. She overcame her fear of flying and was soon able to handle her anger much better. She gained insight regarding her social inhibitions and took positive steps to turn the situation around. Some of the steps that she took will be covered in detail in later chapters on recovery.

Neil

Neil is another interesting example of a person with a performance priority. I am intimately familiar with the details of this case because it is my own story.

To most of the world, I was known as one who was strong and sure. I was an achiever in middle and high school, always bringing home top grades. I tried various outside activities like music and sports. I performed well in these areas but would quickly drop out if I could not be one of the best.

In college, I chose an area of study that had been endorsed by my father as showing the most promise for a productive career with high earnings. I had always been interested in science and wanted to go to medical school but based on my father's recommendation I majored in computer systems engineering.

Again, I brought home top grades in my engineering program. Since mathematics and physics were not personal interests and since I did not have natural ability in these areas, I had to expend a tremendous amount of effort to achieve at a level that was acceptable. Success, even in an area not of personal interest, was enough to keep me going.

I eventually completed the program and took a job in the field of engineering. I repeated my pattern of trying hard and achieving, this time with my career. I would take on the largest and most difficult assignments and bring them to successful conclusion. I gained a reputation as a top engineer and soon as an engineering manager. My life appeared to be what most people consider to be successful.

Unfortunately, as the years progressed into early adulthood, the proverbial wheels fell off in several areas of my life. I had difficulty making personal decisions. When following a methodology at work I could reach decisions because they were scientifically derived. Things would fall into place because of the methods employed. In life things were not as logical. Whether the issue was buying a car or choosing the best underwear, decisions seemed to be a personal struggle. My friends and family would be distressed by what seemed to be endless deliberation.

I was a star player at work but had some weaknesses in that area as well. There were some relatively minor problems that could use some attention like not being flexible in receiving suggestions from others. When it was time to deal with these issues I didn't receive criticism well from my boss. I was a very easy person to talk with but negative feedback about my performance was a hot button that seemed to be impossible to address.

With a rising profile at work, I became a political target. Along with my success came resentment from others and some bitter office struggles. I had always been the kind of person who wanted to please others. With all of the strife in the office I found myself in a position where that was impossible to do. The stress created by this contentious situation eventually caused physical illness in addition to the emotional distress.

If asked, I would have reported that I had a "normal" and good experience in my formative years. Although I would have to be honest and report that I did not have a good experience in elementary school. My first-grade teacher was abusive by any standard. Her harsh and condemning treatment caused me to retreat from the world of learning to a safe place within myself for a period of about six years. A strict hand from my father seemed to awaken me from a deep sleep academically.

To gain a better understanding of how this could affect development it is useful to take a brief look at Erikson's theory (R. Thomas, 1996, McDonald, 2001). Erik Erikson is one of the most respected theorists in the area of human development. In his theory, he proposes that there are several stages of development that children go through organized chronologically by age. At each stage, there are critical personality attributes that are to be assimilated. These are the characteristics that we either carry forward successfully or make compensations for in our efforts to strive for emotional survival in life.

Erikson's Stages

Infant (0 to 1)
Attribute - Trust or mistrust
Virtue - Hope
Needs maximum comfort with minimal
    uncertainty to trust himself/herself, others, and
    the environment.

Toddler (1-3)
Attribute - Autonomy or Shame and Doubt
Virtue – Will
Works to master physical environment while
    maintaining self-esteem.

Preschool (3-5)
Attribute – Initiative or Guilt
Virtue - Purpose
Begins to initiate, not imitate, activities,
develops conscience and sexual identity

School-Age Child (6-11)   ***** Critical Period for a
Performance Priority *****
Attribute – Industry or Inferiority
Virtue - **Competence**
Tries to develop a sense of self-worth by
refining skills

Adolescent (12-18)

Attribute – Identity or Role confusion

Virtue – Fidelity

Tries integrating many roles (child, sibling,
    student, athlete, worker) into a self-image under role
    model and peer pressure.

Young Adult (19-35)

Attribute – Intimacy or Isolation

Virtue – Love

Learns to make personal commitment to
another as spouse, parent or partner

Middle-Age Adult (35 – 50)

Attribute - Generativity or stagnation

Virtue – Care

Seeks satisfaction through productivity in
career, family and civic interests

Maturity (50 +)

Attribute – Ego Integrity or Despair

Virtue – Wisdom

Time of reflection and looking back to evaluate life

If something traumatic happens at one of these stages,
a deficit can be left in our development. The deficit can be in
the form of a hole in one specific area or it can take the shape
of arrested development for the rest of the stages.

From age 6 to age 12 when I was supposed to be developing a healthy sense of competence I switched off and retreated in fear of the potential for further abusive treatment. In terms of Erikson's stages of development, it is conceivable that the personality attribute of having confidence in my own ability to be industrious never developed. If the theory holds true, what was left was a sense of inferiority. When I finally woke up at age 12 to find out that I actually did have academic ability, I made it my quest to rub it in the face of the rest of the world.

I had a good family with no problems like abuse, alcoholism or marital conflict. Unfortunately, receiving personal affirmation and affection from my family was a different story. My mother was very nurturing but my father was under a lot of pressure from his career as an industrial engineer. He was a good provider but was emotionally distant when I was young. Problems were not discussed, especially issues that pertained to personal feelings. It was dangerous to express feelings like anger or frustration because my father was such a large and formidable figure. He stood 6 feet 4 inches tall and weighed over 200 pounds. Affection and affirmation were not freely given. I was continually told that engaging in constructive activities was the best thing that I could do. I was regularly compared to other children that engaged in constructive activities. Eventually I became a very productive student in order to obtain any kind of favorable attention from my father. Producing and being constructive became my way of surviving emotionally. I was attempting to gain favorable attention and overcome deep feelings of inferiority. This emphasis was assimilated in my basic personality and was carried forward into adulthood.

The kind of inner beliefs that were contributing to my misery are as follows:

- Being productive/constructive is the most important aspect of life. I should choose the financially productive career.
- I must make the right decisions/choices. If I fail it is an indication that I do not deserve and will not acquire affirmation as a worthwhile individual.
- I cannot allow anyone to believe that I perform negatively in any area. If I do it is an admission of worthlessness and inadequacy.
- I must please others in my actions. This is how I know that I am performing and that I am acceptable.

By my late twenties, I found myself in a miserable state emotionally. I was in failing health and in a career, that was not suited to my natural interests or abilities. I had no idea how all of this had transpired and knew that it was beyond my personal abilities to fix. In time, I became willing to commit the issue to Christ in an effort to find His way for my life. Obviously, I am no longer in the field of computer engineering. The Lord, as my Wonderful Counselor, has indeed made some changes. Allowing God to rework our souls from the inside out is one of the major areas to be discussed in the chapters on recovery. We will take a look at some of the ways that God moves to initiate the deeply needed changes in our lives.

Chapter 4
The Way Out

It is not God's intention for us to live lives imprisoned by emotional clutter. Looking at this truth in another way, we can say that it is God's will for us to live lives of fulfillment. This fulfillment is acquired by being fully present in our relationships with God and with others. It is fully realized when we are as effective as possible in the missions that He has called us to complete in this life. We cannot be fully present and we cannot be effective in our calling when we see and live life through the filters of faulty belief systems.

Jesus told us that He came so that we might have life and have it more abundantly. He said that He came to set us free. This abundance and freedom that He spoke about is true fulfillment. We need to understand that there is a direct relationship between what plays in our inner belief system and that emotional clutter identified earlier. The emotional clutter gives birth to negative beliefs which in turn give rise to negative behavior. If it is true that He wants fulfillment for us and if it is also true that our faulty inner belief systems are holding us back, then we must find ways to bring about change in those inner belief systems. We must replace what is false with what is true.

This sounds incredibly easy. Simply tell the person who is suffering about the grace of God and about their personal worth as His child and they'll straighten up and fly right. Maybe we should just give them a good smack over the head with a thick King James Bible to get this stuff to sink in.

Unfortunately, some counseling approaches actually take this kind of simplistic approach (just kidding about the Bible smacking). These well-meaning teaching / preaching approaches miss the opportunity for effective ministry. Certainly, making the afflicted person aware of the truth is an important part of the healing process. Remember though, many of the case examples used earlier were about people who already knew what the Bible says about grace and His love for each of us. They didn't have a knowledge deficit. They had a heart deficit. Deep in the innermost parts of their souls something had gone wrong. During their development when strong and secure connections should have been made in the fabrics of their being, stitches were dropped and threads were crossed.

How then do we proceed when the innermost part of our being needs reweaving? First, a personal decision must be made that we really want to proceed. It is much easier and much more comfortable to continue with life thinking that we are okay and that the rest of the world needs to change around us. Personal change is difficult. One good analogy for this threatening situation is the experience of facing a surgical procedure. If you have a cancerous tumor it is inconvenient, difficult and uncomfortable to undergo surgery. If you want to recover from your illness you must make a decision to commit to the process regardless of the discomfort involved.

In many cases, we are not entirely responsible for the difficult situations in life that have contributed to our emotional condition. Earlier we saw how parental injunctions from our childhood can sometimes set the stage for a dysfunctional lifestyle as an adult. It may be true that we cannot be held responsible for the way we were treated as a child but we are responsible as adults for our recovery and continued growth. We can recognize our need and commit our wills to the process of recovery. Blaming others, denying the truth or running in the other direction are all attractive sounding alternatives but they do not lead to recovery and fulfillment.

In general, it is not too difficult to convince the person with a performance priority to commit their will to a task. In working with people trapped by addiction it is not uncommon to discuss the idea of hitting "rock bottom." This is the idea that the afflicted person will have to lose it all in life, hitting rock bottom, before they become willing to face their problem. This may occur with this syndrome as well, but more often there will be an attitude of "What do I have to do to get better?" and "I want it done now rather than later!"

In answer to the question of what to do, you have to be willing to embrace the truth and make yourself available for change. Notice that both of these areas are about willingness and commitment rather than things to do. The performance priority causes the afflicted person to search for a task to complete and an agenda to advance. What we are seeking in recovery is a heart-level change. This change will entail a release of all that the individual holds dear. The things that have been the foundation of the person's soul and have been perceived to be vital to their basic survival must be released. New ways must be embraced.

Chapter 5
Therapeutic Approaches

What follows is a summation of several therapeutic approaches that can bring relief to those afflicted with a performance priority. Conceptually, we are body, mind and spirit. Our starting point is at the level of body and mind. We will be addressing day to day survival first. We are assuming that quite a number of things are out of order in our lives if we have been living with a performance priority. The initial objective is to promote stability with some basic coping mechanisms. Once emotional and behavioral stability is achieved, we are then ready for a more direct attack on the root of the problem. The details of that attack will be covered later.

The information that follows is not intended to be a substitute for actual counseling and therapy. Working with a professional is the best situation. At the same time, understanding what is important to a person afflicted with this condition, we will turn our attention to some things that can be a help right away. Many of these techniques can be self-initiated.

Living a Healthy Life - Realm of the Mind
Stress Reduction

Stress reduction is a key to recovery for persons struggling with a performance priority. Generally, these people have been fighting an up-hill battle on every front of their lives in an attempt to earn their way. We have seen how some have developed anxiety disorders and physical illnesses as a result of living with the tension common in this belief system. It is appropriate to bring the general level of stress down to reduce some of the symptoms and to prepare the way for other modes of healing.

A good resource for a detailed explanation of stress reduction is The Anxiety & Phobia Workbook (Bourne, 1997). This book lists several proven techniques to bring stress under control along with extensive approaches for anxiety disorders. Another detail level source is Stress and Strategies for Lifestyle Management by Kenneth Matheny and Richard Riordan (1992). A more concise and personal treatment of the subject can be found in The Personal Stress Reduction Program by Jeffrey Forman and Dave Meyers (1987).

Controlled Breathing

Breathing is closely associated with your inner tension level. A tense person's breathing is shallow, rapid and occurs in the upper part of the chest. A relaxed person's breathing is deep and from the lower region of the chest. In theory, it is difficult to remain tense and breathe deeply in a controlled manner at the same time.

One simple exercise in controlled breathing is as follows:

1. Breathe from your lower chest
2. Inhale slowly to a count of 5.
3. Pause briefly before exhaling.
4. Exhale slowly to a count of 5.
5. Continue for 3 to 5 minutes.

If you become light headed discontinue the procedure for a few minutes. When you are ready to begin again make sure that you are breathing slowly and in a controlled manner. You should notice a significant reduction in your stress level.

Progressive Muscle Relaxation

This is another proven stress buster. The procedure involves tensing various individual muscle groups in progression. It is proposed that it is difficult to be both anxious and have a relaxed body at the same time. Some other things are at work in this exercise as well. First, the person becomes aware of the difference between a tensed muscle group and a relaxed muscle group. With practice, it becomes more natural to identify tension in everyday situations and intentionally relax. Additionally, the anxious mind is disengaged and focused on other tasks during the exercise.

In order to use this technique, it is a good idea to get into a comfortable position either sitting or lying down. The muscle group is tensed for about 10 seconds then relaxed for 10 to 15 seconds. Notice how the muscles feel when they are tensed and notice how they feel when they are relaxed. Take your time and work through your body systematically (Forehead, eyes, jaw, neck, shoulders, arms, chest, stomach, buttocks, thighs, calf muscles, feet). When you are done, check your muscle groups for tension. If there is any tension present repeat the exercise in that area.

Guided Imagery

The goal of this exercise is to recall a peaceful scene in your mind. Typical scenes are a babbling mountain brook or an ocean beach. The scene should be associated with pleasure and relaxation. If we can successfully recall these memories on command, the sensation of pleasure and relaxation will replace the tension that we are experiencing. It may seem too simple to be effective but this has proven to be an integral part of a number of treatments for anxiety disorders.

It is important to use an image that is personally pleasing and relaxing to you. Recall the experience in all of the detail that you can. Include sounds, smells, tactile feelings (cool, warm, rough, smooth, grainy ...), colors and more.

Biofeedback

This is a technique that has been made possible by advances in computer technology. The proliferation of personal computers has made it more accessible to the general public. In a biofeedback system, the computer monitors body functions associated with the stress response and feeds the results back to the user via sounds or visual graphic displays. All of the monitoring and reporting occurs in real time. This means that information about the subject is captured and reported promptly enough to have significance and potentially an impact on what is happening in real life.

Several body functions can be monitored that relate to the stress response like heart rate, blood pressure, etc. One of these systems, called Freeze Frame, measures heart rhythm (Childre, 1998). These systems provide feedback to the subject regarding the progress of their relaxation response.

When they use a stress reduction technique like imagery or controlled breathing they are immediately informed regarding the effectiveness of their efforts. In principle, the subject learns more quickly what is most effective in controlling their stress level. They are encouraged by the system when they are making positive progress and discouraged when they are not.

A Simple and Effective Technique

There is one more stress reduction technique that I would like to include in this section. It combines some scientifically proven methods with Christian disciplines. It is an approach that I have adapted from the Freeze Frame method. I have incorporated some prayer and Christian imagery. It is called Heart Connection.

Heart Connection

1)   Take a time-out.

2)   Eyes closed and relaxed. Focus on your heart. Take several deep breaths (slowly in, slowly out)

3)   Feel a moment of deep appreciation or love. (God's blessing, ...) Stay here for at least 10 to 15 seconds.

4)   Take the problem that's been in your mind and troubling your heart and give it to the Lord.

5)   Visualize Him standing before you with hands outstretched to receive the problem.

6)   Let go of it! Leave it with Him.

7)   Visualize Him holding His healing palm out to you to comfort your heart regarding this problem.

3)   Check with your heart. Do you have any new insights or new feelings?

A Healthy Life Physically - Realm of the Body

Exercise, diet and healthy sleep habits are key factors in controlling stress. The area of living a healthy lifestyle cannot be covered comprehensively in this work but there are a few thoughts that might be appropriate. It seems that the older we get the wiser our parents get regarding their directions in the area of healthy personal habits. As mom said, in order to feel our best, we must take care of ourselves. Recent studies are confirming the truth of our parents' words.

Sleep

It has been found that an increasing number of Americans are trying to operate in this life with a sleep deficit. This leads to more than just a little irritability. Impairments in judgment and reaction time have been documented in persons attempting to function without an appropriate amount of sleep. If a sleep deficit causes us to perform at a level that is less than our best, what then is the logical result for the one who constantly tries to please others and be his or her best? The outcome can be a pattern of negative thoughts and feelings pertaining to the idea that he or she is not able to earn their rightful place in this world. As these thoughts gain momentum stress builds. The best approach is to stay out of the deficit position in the first place.

The actual amount of sleep that each person requires varies from individual to individual. My own system seems to require eight hours of sleep. Some do well with slightly less. Some need slightly more. The best thing to do is to find out what your own optimum level of rest is and stick to it. It is also a good idea to keep a regular schedule regarding your time of rest. Try to get to bed and rise at the same times each day.

It is a good idea to avoid the inevitable frustration involved with performing beneath our potential, but there is another reason to do a better job in this area of self-care. The primary objective should be to maximize our strength so that we can cope with the challenges of life in the most positive, truthful and rational manner.

Exercise

We are learning more about the importance of exercise from recent research as well. Studies have shown that persons suffering from depression recover better with moderate amounts of physical exercise. It is proposed that exercise has a positive effect on the balance of neurotransmitters in our systems. Some even think that exercise may have a more powerful impact than drug intervention.

Certainly, weight control is much easier if a portion of our caloric intake is used in physical exercise. Our bodies continue to burn calories long after we finish exercising as a result of a higher metabolism rate. There are a number of ways to work some form of exercise into our routine. It doesn't have to be as rigorous as long distance running or pumping iron at the local gym. Just one half hour of brisk walking each day can make a big difference in our health.

Nutrition

Finally, diet and nutrition have a significant impact on our emotional state as well.

One of the more obvious areas that should be addressed is the use of stimulants. Since stress is a physical and emotional reaction to stimulation, it makes good sense to eliminate substances that tend to add more fuel to the fire. Caffeine, nicotine and certain over-the-counter medications can be strong stimulants and their use should be restricted or eliminated.

There are a number of other things that can prove to be stressors on our systems. Sugar, excessive salt intake, preservatives, hormones in meats and food allergies all can prove to be contributors. The best approach is to consult a physician that is well versed in nutrition to provide a personalized set of guidelines.

Just as it is a good practice to eliminate foods and medications that will contribute negatively to stress levels, it is also advisable to be aware of nutrients that make a positive contribution. Recent research is showing that there is a correlation between the level of omega-3 fatty acids (found in some kinds of fish) and depression. The findings demonstrate that patient populations with depression have a lower level of these fatty acids in their systems than control populations. Vitamins are also important when considering stress response. Our systems use B vitamins at a higher rate when we are under stress. Deficiencies in B vitamins can lead to anxiety (Bourne, 1997). Certain minerals are also key players. Calcium and magnesium can be a natural muscle relaxant and act as a kind of tranquilizer.

There are many ways to add these nutrients to our daily diets. One way is to make sure that we are eating the right kinds of foods. The other is to use natural vitamin supplements. Sometimes making changes in both areas is advisable. Certain herbs can have beneficial effects in reducing stress. As with all of the aspects of self-care (sleep, exercise and nutrition) it is best to consult a physician who has specific training in these areas. He or she will be able to help plan any changes and make sure that your approach is safe and appropriate for your needs, especially if you choose to use herbal supplementation. Certain herbs can cause problems when taken in combination with other medications.

A Healthy Life in the Realm of the Spirit
Prayer and Meditation

It is important to note that regular prayer and meditation are generally accepted as effective methods for stress reduction (Propst, 1988). In his book Psychology, Theology, and Spirituality in Christian Counseling (1996), Mark McMinn supports the effectiveness of these two Christian disciplines. One of the research projects he cites is concerned with the effectiveness of intercessory prayer. In that double-blind study, a number of the recipients of prayer were healthier on hospital discharge than the control group. The probability of error or random occurrence in the results was less than one in ten thousand. McMinn goes on to explain that devotional meditation has also been a topic of research. Some of these studies have shown meditation to be at least as effective as progressive relaxation in reducing anxiety and anger. Employing these two disciplines on our own and enlisting the support of other members of the body of Christ for prayer is a good prescription for healing.

Recently one of my counseling clients described prayer as something that was necessary. I asked her if that was like saying that talking to your husband is *necessary*. I would hope that talking to your husband is enjoyable, rejuvenating, and a source of strength. Our connection to God is our connection to sanity, peace, love and power in an otherwise insane and treacherous world. To neglect that connection is to cut off our own air supply.

Know the Truth – Reading God's Word

Taking time to read God's word is certainly important to Christians who are recovering from stress related conditions. How many times has God encouraged us from His Word to "fear not" and to "be not anxious ...." We need to remind ourselves of His faithfulness and His love for us on a regular basis.

Some of my favorites of the many scriptures that pertain to stress and anxiety:

Do not be afraid of sudden fear nor of the onslaught of the wicked when it comes; for the Lord will be your confidence and will keep your foot from being caught. Proverbs 3:25&26

...casting all your anxiety on Him, because He cares for you. 1 Peter 5: 7

Be anxious for nothing, but in everything by prayer and supplication with thanksgiving let your requests be made known to God. Philippians 4: 6

Staying Connected – Being in His Presence

When we lose the connection to our Maker the door is left open to the insecure feelings of being alone in a dangerous world. Taking time to be in God's presence is a key to our survival. Jesus said that He was going to the Father so that the Helper would come (John 16:7). He was speaking of the Holy Spirit. If we are not taking time to connect in real relationship with Him, we are missing something critical that Jesus intended for us. The Holy Spirit's ministry is to bring comfort in our time of need, to enable us to transcend the difficulties in this imperfect world and to empower us to fulfill our personal missions in His service. We will go into more detail about spiritual growth and healing as a part of what was mentioned earlier about a more direct attack on the performance priority.

There are many good resources that are useful in learning about spiritual growth. The book by this writer entitled Memoirs from the Rear Pew (2002, 2017) traces the process of spiritual growth from the perspective of an ordinary person. Too often we feel that spiritual growth and fulfillment is only for special people like Billy Graham or the pastor of our church. This book is a personal testimony to the faithfulness of God as evidenced in the life experiences of an ordinary person.

If you are not sure about your spiritual condition or want to know more about spiritual growth, Christian books like this one are helpful. It is also a good idea to get connected to a healthy Christian congregation. In order to grow we need to be exposed to God's word in many forms. Preaching and teaching, the kind that is true to what is written in the Bible, is critical. The support and fellowship that can be found in a church congregation can also make an important contribution to our well-being. Researchers in the area of effective counseling and therapy are recognizing the powerful force that a positive congregation can be in the life of a person in need of emotional strength.

Warning Concerning Counterfeits

There are many good things in this world for which there are counterfeit copies. The church is not an exception. We should be aware of these counterfeits and steer a wide course around them. There are many congregations and leaders who look as though they are spiritual or religious but are actually inspired by human or satanic ambition. Just as there are abusive families that cause human suffering and destruction, there are abusive religious leaders and organizations. Some of these are easily identifiable as cults in their controlling techniques. Some are almost undetectably subtle in their advancement of erroneous teachings. These are teachings that enslave their members in legalistic rules that only sound religious. Teaching according to the truth of the gospel sets people free. The apostle Paul had some pretty strong words for some teachers that were trying to enslave the Galatians. In that situation circumcision was being added to the list of religious requirements for Christians and Paul was absolutely beside himself. According to Paul the Galatians had forgotten that they had been saved by grace. His statements were very direct and to the point.

> It was for freedom that Christ set us free; therefore, keep standing firm and do not be subject to a yoke of slavery. Galatians 5: 1

> You have been severed from Christ, you who are seeking to be justified by law; you have fallen from grace. Galatians 5: 4

> ... but the one who is disturbing you will bear his judgment ... Galatians 5: 10

> I wish that those who are troubling you would even mutilate themselves. Galatians 5: 12

I'm thankful for Paul's boldness and his enthusiasm for the spiritual health of that early church. In retrospect, I believe that Paul would agree with some additional thoughts. Even though Paul had those angry wishes regarding the perpetrators, he would agree that the right thing to do is to pray for those leaders who are in error. Pray also that their influence over innocent Christians will be broken. For your personal well-being, it is a good idea to stay clear of their negative influence and teachings.

Great care should be taken to be sure that the initial feelings of acceptance by a group or a leader does not cloud our judgment. It is likely that the person with a performance priority has suffered from some sort of an "acceptance deficit" in the past. They adopted the performance priority as their way of compensating. When leaders or groups make their appeal as someone who genuinely cares for you, it is powerful and difficult to resist.

Use a spiritual appraisal checklist:

- Does the leader or group lift up Jesus Christ? (That He is Lord and Savior)
- Does what they say agree with what is in God's word? (His whole word, not just portions of scripture taken out of context)
- What is your inner witness (the guidance of the Holy Spirit) telling you?
- What is the general witness of the rest of the body of Christ regarding this person or group?

Satan and a great many human sponsored systems would like nothing better than for us to forfeit our freedom so that they can gain control. Sometimes the subtle human objective of erroneous leaders is to feel justified themselves. Leaders who depend on something other than grace to feel justified feel a personal boost when their own erroneous approach is accepted and put into practice by their flock. It may sound ridiculous to think that a Christian leader would do such a thing when they are supposed to be the purveyors of grace. Remember that the performance priority is usually outside of our consciousness. If these leaders developed in a family system that gave rise to a performance priority it is likely that the tendency will spill over into their relationship with God and their teaching of others. If deep in their belief systems they think that they must do something to obtain attention, love, grace, etc. then they will act and teach that way as well.

There are a number of good references on abusive systems. One good one is <u>The Subtle Power of Spiritual Abuse</u> (1991) by David Johnson and Jeff VanVonderen. Another is <u>When God's People Let You Down</u> by Jeff VanVonderen (1995). These works go into detail explaining the dangers of spiritual abuse. A summary of things to watch out for is as follows:

- Shame based systems - Considerable guilt and shame are inflicted on those that transgress the rules of the system.
- Closed systems – All authority comes from within the system. All outside influences are discounted as inferior, wrong or evil.
- No talk rules – It is assumed that one is not to speak out. Leaders are often not available to deal with issues.
- Blame is turned on the injured – When an issue is brought out, the defense tactic is to turn the blame back on the injured party. (We'll just pray for your critical spirit!)
- Emphasis on self-denial and legalism – Great sacrifices of time and resources are seen as the road to spiritual growth.

Spiritual abuse is more common that one might think. For that reason, it is important for everyone to be as informed as possible regarding the tell-tale signs and negative effects.

Page 57

Perhaps the healthy approach can be summarized by saying that grace plus anything else is not grace! Any message that is counter to grace is to be avoided. The person with a performance priority has an internal belief system that is the antithesis of grace to begin with. It is for that reason that it is so important to become a part of a church that teaches the truth about freedom in Jesus Christ. Find a church where you feel that freedom. If you find that your joy is gone, the joy that you felt when you first came to Christ, it may be because of subtle forms of spiritual abuse. Abuse can be from forces that are malicious or from forces that are totally convinced that their approach is correct. In any case, be aware of what spiritual abuse is all about. Pray that the Lord would lead you to the right church home and then don't hesitate to use good spiritual appraisal techniques. Living a healthy life spiritually is a foundational element in having peace in our hearts and minimizing stress. Use all the resources at your disposal, but choose them wisely.

So far, what has been discussed regarding "the way out" of life with a performance priority has been concerned with house cleaning. Our objective has been to make our lives ready for change. We have looked at the importance of stress reduction and living a healthy life both physically and spiritually.

Conforming to all of these guidelines may seem like a lot to ask. Some readers may have already dropped out because it seems to be too much. Remember what was said earlier about the importance of your initial decision to commit to change. A performance priority doesn't make a minor difference in your life. It can actually dominate in every area, bringing illness and misery. Big problems require big commitments. I encourage you to press on making small steps toward your goal. Don't give up because it seems too hard. Housekeeping is not a job that we complete all at once. It seems that there is always more to do. Even so, we can get better in our efforts in a step-by-step fashion. Make some small and attainable changes, never taking your eyes off the final goal of reclaiming your life from bondage to the terrible taskmaster of performance.

If we are doing all that we can to make ourselves ready for change, what then can we do to directly deal with the problem of a performance priority?

What follows is the more "direct attack" on the problem that was mentioned earlier. You may recall that the core of the issue is a faulty belief system. The next chapter goes further in the realm of the mind, detailing several psychological approaches that can be used to promote recovery.

Chapter 6
Assimilating New Ways of Thinking

Albert Ellis and Aaron Beck are revered as two of the pioneers in the field of cognitive-behavioral therapy. They have been given credit for originating many of the principles and theories of this school of psychology. What most people don't know is that God has been on top of that approach for quite some time. The cognitive theorists say that a person's thoughts influence behavior. God has said in His Word, "For as he thinks within himself, so he is." Proverbs 23:7

The principle that our thoughts and beliefs influence our lives is not a new one. It follows that if God has known this all along, perhaps there are other truths from His tool kit that can help. Man has discovered a number of God's truths through scientific research. Many of these truths have given rise to therapeutic approaches that have proven to be effective. The integrative approach to Christian counseling combines those scientific approaches with the underlying truths from God's Word to facilitate the healing process.

The ABC's of Recovery

Albert Ellis (Corey, 1996) uses the first three letters of the alphabet to explain the basic principles of his cognitive (based on thoughts) approach to understanding human behavior.

Ellis's ABC's - Definitions:

    A → Activating event

    B → Inner belief about the event

    C → Consequence that results or our emotional reaction.

Let's use the example of an interfering mother-in-law as our activating event and anger as the consequence. Most of us would say our mother-in-law makes us angry. This is illustrated as follows:

    A → C

Ellis would maintain that it is not your mother-in-law that makes you angry. In actuality it is your belief about your mother-in-law. The diagram looks like this:

    A → B → C

The belief might be that she interferes just to make your life miserable. It could be something as simple as thinking that her interference is terrible and that you can't stand it. The activating event (A) is filtered through your inner belief system (B), which actually influences your emotional consequences (C).

It might be quite an eye opener to discover that it is not your mother-in-law that bothers you after all. All along it has been what you believe about her that is really causing the rub. If that's really true then it follows that changing your belief system will influence your emotional consequences or reactions in life. This takes us back to the idea of commitment. It is within your power to do something about your negative emotions. If you really want to reclaim that part of your life you must make the personal choice to change. Once you're ready the next challenge is to find out how to influence those belief systems.

Ellis suggests starting by tracking back from our negative emotional reactions to the activating events. Recognizing your reaction, ask yourself what belief might have caused you to respond in that way. Once you have identified the irrational thought it must be challenged. Ask yourself what evidence you have that this belief is true. Next, the truth must be put in place of the irrational belief. If might work something like this:

1. <u>Acknowledge your emotional reaction</u>.
I am getting angry with that no-good mother-in-law of mine.

2. <u>Commit to Change</u>.
Since I have decided that I don't want to be a victim of my negative emotional outbursts anymore, I will challenge my thinking about her.

3. <u>Identify the Irrational Thought</u>
What have I been thinking when she does this?
I might be thinking that she **shouldn't** try to make me miserable and that I just **can't** stand it.

4. <u>Challenge the Irrational Thought</u>
What evidence do I have that she really is trying to make me miserable?
Is it really true that she **shouldn't** act this way?
What makes me think that I **can't** stand her bad behavior?

5. <u>Put the Truth in Place of the Irrational Thought</u>
I know that she learned to act this way from her mother and she is behaving in the only way that she knows. She is just an imperfect human being.

I know that I can endure her bad behavior if needed.

What is truthful is that I would **prefer** that my mother-in-law not misbehave. I would **rather** not have to experience the distress but I certainly **can** live through it so that I can find a better way.

Ellis's method provides some additional guidance to help identify irrational thoughts and beliefs. Thinking in absolute terms is a clue that our thinking needs some adjustment. Terms like **should**, **must** and **can't** are tips that we are headed in the wrong direction.

He also lists a trilogy of non-functional beliefs that he considers to be common in our society:

*1.I **should** be perfectly competent and masterful, and I am a worthless individual if I am not.*

This might be the most prevalent silent thought that is playing in the minds of persons with a performance priority. It is probably their subconscious life-slogan.

*2.Others **should** treat me considerately and fairly, and if they don't, they are rotten people.*

The person with a performance priority believes this way because they try to make their way in this world by acting considerately and fairly. If they do these things all the time then others **should** also!

*3.The world **should** arrange for me to experience pleasure rather than pain, and life is horrible and I **can't** stand it if the world doesn't.*

This is also a dangerous thought for persons suffering with this affliction. The belief is something like the following. If the world doesn't deliver after all that I have done and continue to do, then life is truly horrible. I know it is horrible because I haven't a clue what to do differently. The reaction is usually anger followed by depression.

Aaron Beck, the second cognitive theorist mentioned earlier, made some interesting statements concerning types of distortions in thinking. Many of these play an active part in the belief systems of those afflicted by a performance priority.

1. *Perfectionistic thinking*

This is the belief that nothing short of perfect performance is worthwhile. While we have seen that a performance priority is more than perfectionism, it is easy to understand how this kind of thinking can take hold in this situation. Performance earns my position, so I want nothing less than perfect performance.

2. *Personalization*

With this kind of thinking the person inappropriately assumes responsibility for external events. In our case examples, Patty took responsibility for everything and everyone. She would gladly do so because it gave her an opportunity to earn her position in this world thereby bringing her a sense of self-worth.

3. *Overgeneralization*

People conclude that because they have failed today in a specific area, they will never be able to succeed in life. This is proof to themselves that their efforts do not bring the expected results. The response is to give up.

4. *Polarized thinking or All-or-Nothing thinking*

The person with a performance priority might believe that, because there was one critical remark on their performance review, the review was horrible and it is an indication of their complete failure.

If we accept the idea that our thinking determines who we are, then all of these distortions in thinking must be stopped. The Bible addresses the idea of stopping bad thoughts in 2nd Corinthians.

We are taking every thought captive to the obedience of Christ. 2nd Corinthians 10:5

All of the distorted thinking that is playing in our minds and troubling our hearts must be identified as irrational and taken captive. We take the bad thoughts captive by challenging them rationally. Ask yourself if the thought makes sense logically. Is there evidence to support that thought? Does that thought match up with what we know to be true in God's word?

If you find that the thought is not true, take action to replace it with something that is true. The Bible supports this approach in Philippians.

Finally, brethren, whatever is true, whatever is honorable, whatever is right, whatever is pure, whatever is lovely, whatever is of good repute, if there is any excellence and if anything is worthy of praise, dwell on these things. Philippians 4:8

The temptation is to wait until your feelings change before you take action. If we accept the idea that the belief is the mediator that is directly influencing our emotions (B → C), then the feelings are not likely to change without an action that has an impact on the belief. Feelings might subside temporarily if you avoid contact with your mother-in-law. Although research has shown that avoidance gives rise to perceptions of dominance in relationships (Olson, 1998). You may begin to feel more resentful toward her behavior as you believe that her actions put her more and more in control. You might feel better temporarily if you lash out aggressively with some harsh words or actions. Later you are likely to feel worse about what you did or suffer the consequences of serious damage to relationships. Both avoiding and being aggressive end in self-generated defeat. What is needed is positive action based upon truth not a warm fuzzy feeling. Action based on truth will empower you to behave in a way that is uplifting not self-defeating. The objective is more than obtaining a temporary reprieve or venting an impulsive emotion. Real change makes you stronger in the challenging situations of life and makes it possible for you to transcend the issues that previously ended in defeat. Real change means that there is something new and fundamentally different in your heart that you will carry forward for the rest of your life. The process is like building a new and firmer foundation from which you can draw strength to face life's challenges head-on.

The Real "Magic"

My grandmother was a purveyor of practical wisdom. I loved and respected her very much and her words seemed to have magical power. She used to say, "We can talk about it until the cows come home, talking doesn't mean anything unless you do something." She knew that action is the key ingredient if there is any "magic formula" for real change. Behavior seems to turn a key in our hearts regarding the assimilation of new beliefs. There is a progression of positive action that is at play in this assimilation process.

1. Recognize a concept   Learning
2. Embrace it   Faith
3. Take action on it (Risk)   Trust

First, we have to know what the truth is in order to make some positive changes. We can gain insight in a number of ways. As with all aspects of recovery, there must be an open mind and a willingness to participate. Insight can be gained independently through research, studying the scriptures or listening to solid teaching. Another way to get the process started is to work with a counselor.

The next step is to make a conscious choice to accept a concept. This is an act of the will and it requires a level of faith. Faith is defined in the Bible as:

... a hope in something unseen Hebrews 11:1

Allowing ourselves to have hope in something unseen or unproven gives us a kind of energy or permission to feel

Page 67

differently. Since cognitions (thoughts) are a form of behavior (inner activity), this step is where change begins to happen. You "play new messages" in your mind intentionally. The connection between what you think and who you are takes hold.

For as a man thinks within himself, so he is. Proverbs 23:7

The new thoughts begin to mediate (A→**B**→C) in a more positive way.

In the third step of the assimilation process we are putting more skin in the game. When we take action on a concept we are taking ownership of an issue in a bigger way than just knowing about it and accepting it in our mind. If we come to have a level of belief in a concept and then stake a part of our lives on it by doing something, we are in effect exercising our inner faith. That exercise proves to us experientially that the concept is really true. That proof builds our level of trust. What we trust in is really where we live emotionally. Those things that we have come to trust in are made a part of us for our own survival. They are assimilated and carried forward as part of our personality precipitating lasting change.

An example of taking action with new behavior would be to do something differently concerning your mother-in-law based on your new belief system. If you accept the idea that she is behaving out of her limited set of communication skills and that she is an imperfect human being, then what can you do differently? One option is to pray for her. This sounds like a fairly standard Christian recommendation. Actually, it is something that is very difficult to do when you have been angry with someone. Perhaps you should tell her that you care about her and want to hear how she really feels. This suggestion sounds like doing the exact opposite of what you have been feeling. All along you have wanted either to run in the other direction or take a swing at her. Your new belief system doesn't match up with those feelings. You have to make a conscious decision to act on the new belief system, trusting that it is true. When you do that, you will surprise yourself with your new feelings of empathy and your behavior will certainly be a surprise to your mother-in-law.

When you go through a process like this you are actively living the truth instead of distortions and lies. When you live the truth, you are in a better position to see things as Christ sees them. When you act empathetically toward you mother-in-law you clear away your own personal emotional clutter, put truth in its place and take the vantage point of Christ. From that vantage point it is much easier to act in a loving and giving way rather than acting negatively out of your personal pain. The truly amazing thing is that when you do these things your heart begins to change and you actually feel the love and peace that go along with your new actions.

What we have seen is that a good approach to recovery includes changes in thinking and changes in behavior. Learning about something from a book or from therapy day on Oprah can be helpful but positive steps must be made like actually embracing the truth. This must be followed by taking new action if your goal is to bring about real change.

Taking a Deeper Look at Recovery

To this point in our look at the process of assimilating new ways of thinking we have seen how it is important to identify, challenge and replace irrational thoughts. To make truthful concepts a part of who we are we must take action. This action involves accepting the truth and then taking positive steps in our lives.

Understanding the recovery process as described so far helps to map out a direction for our efforts to improve our lives. We have an idea of where to start and how to proceed along the path to recovery. Unfortunately, there are certain situations that can be real roadblocks to getting started.

One roadblock is a severe level of emotional distress. If you are in an unstable place emotionally as with major depression or anxiety, it is difficult to implement any process or plan. In this situation, it is best to work with a qualified therapist who can facilitate a return to emotional stability. There are times when medications can help to promote stability and make the afflicted person more ready to make life changes.

Another area that can form a roadblock is trauma. According to the Adaptive Information Processing model (Shapiro, 2001), traumatic events can remain locked in our memory in a neurologically disturbing state. Information pertaining to the original event is stored in the form of images, sounds, affect (emotions), and physical sensations. Perhaps the best illustration of this problem is the person suffering from Post-Traumatic Stress Disorder (PTSD). War veterans or disaster victims will sometimes carry the memory of their negative experience with them with disabling results. They may have recurring nightmares. Their behavior might include being highly anxious, hyper-vigilant and emotionally distant. They may be easily triggered into flashbacks of their original painful experience. Although most of us do not experience PTSD symptoms, it has been proposed that many of us do carry with us painful memories that have not been fully resolved. These memories may continue to shape our behavior in self-defeating ways. In these situations, an appropriately trained therapist can facilitate the healing process and break through these kinds of blocks. EMDR (Eye Movement Desensitization and Reprocessing) is a therapeutic technique that has been proven by research to be very effective in providing relief from these problems. If you feel that this may be beneficial to you, a reference list of trained EMDR therapists in your area can be found on the internet at www.emdr.com.

Another roadblock occurs when the irrational belief systems seem elusive. Earlier it was noted that much of the belief system that makes up the performance priority actually resides in an area of our thinking that is beyond our reach. Working with a qualified therapist to learn more about ourselves can help uncover those illusive belief systems. If we know more about how our personalities are wired, we are in a better position to identify beliefs that could be causing trouble. There are a number of approaches that trained therapists use to promote insight and understanding in their clients. These approaches vary depending on the specific theoretical school of psychology of the individual therapist. Some of these approaches include temperament analysis, personality typing, early memory identification, genograms, birth order, family sculptures, and numerous other assessment techniques.

It is beyond the scope of this book to explain the theoretical basis for these techniques, nor is it possible to explain in detail how they are implemented. It is probably enough to note that these approaches are supported by scientific research. Working with tools like these in therapy can reveal a great deal about ourselves that we might never be able to discover by any other means.   Armed with that information we are better prepared to challenge and modify our inner belief systems.

Chapter 7
Adopting New Ways of Behaving

To this point our attack on the performance priority and its associated misery has included reducing stress level, restructuring thoughts and taking positive steps to act in new ways. There are some other topics in the area of behaving differently that can also be helpful. These topics fall into the category the human mind and address some new and more truthful ways of relating to others.

Assertiveness

When your inner belief system tells you that you must perform in a certain way to earn your place or when it tells you that you must please others, your personal needs can take a back seat. Unmet personal needs generate internal stress. The normal human reaction to stressful events is to avoid them or to strike out in anger. Both of these responses are negative. The avoidant response only delays the problem until life brings it around again. We have also discussed how avoiding in relationships can lead to perceptions that you are being dominated by the other person. Striking out in anger aggressively might get your point across but you are not likely to maintain positive relationships for long. Using assertiveness rather than avoiding or being aggressive is a way to channel energy in a positive way, meeting the problem head-on. Communicating your personal needs in a positive way assertively increases the probability of having your needs met.

One way to act assertively is to employ a three-step approach to keep yourself on a positive track. The steps are fairly simple.

1. Acknowledge the other person.
2. State the problem in heart words
3. Make a suggestion

Step #1   Acknowledge the other person in some way.

In this step, you are approaching the person for the first time regarding an issue. Your goal is to engage them in the conversation. You don't want to make them angry before you have a chance to work on the problem. Saying something positive about the other person disarms them in a way. When someone comes up to you and starts the conversation by saying something good about you, you are naturally drawn in. It is best to convey a level of understanding about their position. What could be nicer than hearing that someone really understands you?

In the case of the nasty mother-in-law you might say something like the following.

Mom, I know how much you really care about us.

Or

Mom, I understand how much you love the kids and are concerned for their well-being.

When your feelings are hurt or you are angry with someone it is very hard to start with a positive statement about them. Remember that you are intentionally adopting a new behavior in the hope of avoiding negative emotions and self-defeat.

Step #2   State the problem in terms of your feelings.

This is the most difficult and probably the most critical of the steps. It is easy to go off track and derail the process. The most common way to go off track is to use "**you** language" in your description of the problem. Using the word "you" is usually taken as an attack and puts the person on the defensive.   It is easy to slip into something like this:

Mom, **you** always seem to want to tell us what to do with our time.

Or

Mom, **you** get too involved with the children. **You** make me so mad.

Any form of critical dialog at this point is counterproductive.

It is best to use "I language" as much as possible. The goal is to communicate the problem in terms of your feelings. It could go something like this:

Mom, **I feel** upset and hurt during our conversations about how we spend our time.

Or

Mom, **I feel** so unimportant and invisible when decisions are made about the kids without my input.

By approaching the other person in this way, you are taking a chance. Your hope is that by opening your heart to them they will accept the invitation to help you. Your angry feelings tell you that the other person is wrong and that he or she is really the one that needs the help. Turning the tables and acting this way, regardless of your feelings toward the other person, is non-threatening and continues the process of pulling them into the negotiation to meet your needs. You are taking a chance because your honest, heart-level appeal might be disregarded or attacked. It is hurtful when that happens, but you can stand firm in the confidence that you are approaching them from the standpoint of truth and you are acting in a positive way. If all your attempts at being assertive fail and the person continues to violate areas of your life, there is another path to follow in the area of setting personal boundaries that will be discussed later.

This second step is critical and worth the risk because it opens the door to a level of intimacy that would normally remain closed. You are inviting the person to minister to your heart not just to work on the logistics of the problem. It may seem inconceivable, but wouldn't it be great to have that kind of loving relationship with all the people that are important to us?

Step #3   Make a suggestion

By this time, you have the other person's positive interest and attention. Hopefully they have been empathetically pulled into your world by your honest communication of heart-level needs. Now it is time to propose a possible solution or method to reach a solution. It might look like this:

Mom, I believe it would be best to let me use my own judgment to set my schedule. It will be less of a worry and I will be able to take more responsibility for my life as an adult.

Or

Mom, I really think that we should sit down and discuss the best times to see the kids each week.

Using an assertive approach will improve the lines of communication between you and the rest of the world. The chances of getting your needs met will go way up. The choice is yours. You can choose frustration through avoidance, pain and loss through aggression or satisfaction through assertiveness. It seems like an easy choice. In actuality, adopting new behaviors is difficult no matter how sensible they may seem.   Start by committing your will to the new direction. Make the decision that this is indeed the way that is best. Then practice until it becomes second nature to you. Just as a professional tennis player hits a certain stroke over and over again until it becomes "grooved" in their game, use this method until it becomes a part of you.   When it does, you will feel better about yourself and about the challenging people in your life.

Boundaries

Another major topic in the area of adopting new ways of behaving is setting personal boundaries. Personal boundaries are principles that you adopt to set limits on others. They are like protective fencing that define to what extent others can move into or have influence on your life. A reference that I often recommend to my clients on this topic is the book Boundaries by Cloud and Townsend (1992). This is a good resource for those who would like a detailed explanation of what boundaries are and how they should be used in personal relationships. For the purposes of our discussion of the performance priority there are a few major points regarding boundaries that are important.

Earlier it was mentioned that there are times when challenging people in our lives do not respond to assertive approaches. They persist in their bad behavior, violating things that are of value to us personally. Sometimes the violations are about material things like money, cars or space in the office. Sometimes they are about emotional things like your worth as a spouse or your value as a human being. In cases like this it is important to know how to set personal boundaries to provide protection from continued assaults.

A simple way to start is to decide what things are important to you. Then decide to what extent you will allow others to move into or have influence over those things. Once you have decided how far they can go before there is a violation, draw a boundary line (principle that sets a limit) that is not to be crossed. It is up to you to be vigilant and protect those boundaries once they are set. You can use your assertive communication style to effectively state where your boundaries are to challenging others. Again, with this approach you are coming from the strong position of truth.

It is up to you to enforce the new boundary lines. Don't expect others to be pleased when they run up against a new boundary. It is common for others to push back in an attempt to regain the control or access that they once had. Tell yourself that your objective is not to please others, but to stand up for the truth. By taking that stand you are respecting yourself and taking action on the belief that it is your decision to do so. Your level of self-esteem will begin to build and many times (not always) others will respect your newfound strength as well. Be prepared to follow through with a reasonable and natural consequence when violations occur. Setting a boundary has no effect unless you are vigilant to protect it. A boundary violation with the troublesome mother-in-law might unfold something like this:

Mom, I know that you remember the positive discussion we had last week about the children's playtime on Saturday. It was decided that you would bring them back promptly by 12:00 noon. Since you have continued to disregard our agreement, the kids will have to see you here next week so that I can be assured that they will be home on time.

In this case, the boundary had been set using assertive communication the week before. The perpetrator persisted in the violating behavior. The behavior was met with affirmative action and natural consequences were invoked. For the purposes of this discussion the term natural consequence is being used to mean that the consequence is logically associated with the violation. For example, it would not be natural or productive to tell your mother-in-law that due to her violation you will be letting the air out of her tires. In order to adequately protect your boundaries, you will have to be prepared to escalate your response with increasingly firm natural consequences as appropriate to the situation.

Boundaries and the Performance Priority

People with a performance priority have a low level of self-esteem. Their self-worth is defined by their ability to perform tasks or to please others. With a low level of self-esteem, it is not surprising to find that things of personal value are not always protected. In some cases, there are very few

Page 79

personal boundaries and little skill in the area of establishing them. In the case of Patty, discussed earlier, boundaries seemed to be non-existent. Her family members moved in and out of her life at will. With the overriding objective of pleasing and serving others, Patty's personal needs always took a secondary position. People in her family expected and took more and more from her in the areas of finances, her time and her attention. She continued to give because her performance priority wired her to do so. Stress accumulated to the point that she was losing more than just time and money. She almost lost her health and ultimately her life as well. Fortunately for Patty, she learned to establish some reasonable boundaries in her life. She began to understand her worth as a human being in terms of how God views her as His child. As she began to care for herself as well as she cared for her family members a new strength and confidence could be seen in her.

Learning to love and respect yourself is an important step in becoming able to set appropriate boundaries. One psychological approach for boosting self-esteem is to use self-affirmation statements. These are statements that attest to our worth as human beings. The idea is to repeat these statements to ourselves until they begin to penetrate our belief system. I like to combine this approach with some of the things that we know are true from God's word. One of my favorites is from Psalms.

For you formed my inward parts; You wove me in my mother's womb. I will give thanks to You, for I am fearfully and wonderfully made; wonderful are your works and my soul knows it very well. Psalms 139:13

I like to recommend that the client put this verse on 3 by 5 cards and tape them in prominent places where they will see them throughout the day. A bathroom mirror or the dashboard of the car works nicely.

Once we acknowledge our own worth as a human being we can begin to set some reasonable boundaries for others. The idea is to decide what is reasonable (treating yourself with respect) then to become vigilant in guarding those boundaries. When others attempt to violate a boundary be ready to stand firm in your position. Decide ahead of time what natural consequences are appropriate for violations, then enforce them with confidence.

Finding out that you can set a personal boundary successfully can bring a tremendous sense of freedom. One of my clients recently shared an interesting account of her first experience with boundaries. This woman was in her mid 50's and had survived a number of very difficult relationships in her life. The pattern of destruction and pain in relationships had become pervasive and it seemed to her that there was no escape. By the time she decided to come for counseling, she had developed symptoms of stress and anxiety. She was willing to do whatever it took to break out of her painful existence. In spite of all of the trials, her intelligence, courage and what some call "heart" led me to believe that she would make rapid progress. During one of our sessions the concept of personal boundaries was introduced. The book Boundaries, mentioned earlier, was assigned as homework.

When she came in for her session the next week she had an impish grin on her face. She looked like a kid who had

just stolen the last cookie in the jar without her mom seeing her. She told me that one of her abusive family members had called her on the phone a few nights before. He began his usual behavior of launching verbal assaults telling her how she should run her life. At that point, she said that something new just came out of her mouth. She heard herself giving firm notice of where her personal boundary was. Specifically, she told him that he had no business telling her what to do in that area. When she finished the story her eyes got wide and she smiled at what she had done. It was like she had breathed fresh air for the first time in her life. She knew that she was headed in the right direction.

Knowing the truth, embracing the truth and then being willing to walk in the truth (new behavior) is the progression of change that we have discussed to this point. We have covered several things that we can do as human beings to promote inner healing and change in the areas of the human mind and body.

There is another important source of healing and growth that is a major part of the direct attack on a performance priority. This is the process of spiritual growth and healing. This area was discussed briefly in our look at things that can be done to promote healthy living. At this point we need to go into a little more detail in order to understand how this process works. Spiritual growth and healing is a gift of God that is intended for all of his people. We can't control this gift but we can do some things to make ourselves available to receive it. The realm of the spirit is the next area of focus.

Chapter 8
Spiritual Growth and Healing

A person could read about spiritual growth and healing for a lifetime and still feel that there is more to know. Many books have been written and sermons preached dedicated to this one topic. For the purposes of this discussion, we will focus on how spiritual growth and healing can be an influence in the lives of those affected by a performance priority.

We will be making a few assumptions about spiritual growth. First, we will assume that the nature of spiritual growth, in Christian terms, has to do with relationship. It will be our position that Christianity is more than conforming to a set of religious rules or theological beliefs. Specifically, it will be shown that spiritual growth is the process of building a relationship with the Living God.

In the Beginning

As with all relationships there is a beginning. There is an introduction, an acknowledgment of the other and then a commitment by both parties. The Bible explains this aspect of the spiritual growth process as being born again. This is the idea that we are to be born not only of the flesh but of the Spirit. The Bible teaches that by this process we can know that we have eternal life. A simple prayer of commitment might go something like this:

1. Lord Jesus, I know that you are God's Son and that You sacrificed your life to save me from my sins.

2. I am a sinner, and ask for your forgiveness for all my sins.

3. I invite you into my life and into my heart as my Lord and my Savior.

4. Thank you, Lord for your faithfulness and Your provision of life for me.

This simple commitment sets in motion a life that is brand new in God's Spirit.

Therefore, if any man is in Christ, he is a new creature; the old things passed away; behold, new things have come. 2 Corinthians 5: 17

This first step can be particularly challenging for the one influenced by a performance priority. In this belief system, it is difficult to conceive of a good reason why we should be forgiven and accepted unconditionally. We hear the words of the message of truth but have been wired in our souls to believe that everything is contingent on our own performance. There is a search for a good reason for God's salvation rather than a natural acceptance of His act of grace (unmerited favor). If we have not experienced grace in our early development it will seem like an interesting idea, not something that is a part of our soul already. We form our early concepts about who God is by our experience with our earthly parents. If they did not convey the concept of grace, there will be a deficit in our understanding of the nature of God in our life as an adult.

It is my belief that God works diligently by His Spirit to bring those affected by developmental deficits to a place where they can make a commitment to Him. By His diligent work and with no small amount of struggle, a miracle happens and the relationship begins. The difficulty with the concept of grace is likely to surface again because the intention is not for the introduction and commitment step to be the end of the experience. This is to be an on-going relationship and, as such, it is intended to develop and deepen. This development of the relationship is what we think of as spiritual growth. During the course of that growth, heart deficits like difficulty with the concept of grace are gradually healed as He proves Himself to be faithful. It is a gradual process of letting go of the old beliefs and living according to the new ones.

A relationship can be thought of as kind of a concept. It is a concept we form that pertains to the nature of our interaction with another. If relationship is indeed a form of a concept then it follows that in order for it to become a part of us and grow it would have to go through the three-step assimilation process that we identified earlier for concepts or beliefs. You may have noticed from our earlier review of assimilation that the process sounds very much like something you may have heard before in a sermon or read in your Bible.

In order to assimilate a concept or relationship and make it part of us, we go through the following steps:

1. Recognize a concept   Learning
2. Embrace it   Faith
3. Take action   Trust

In the prayer of commitment outlined above all of the three steps are taken. There is recognition of a truth (understanding), a choice to accept (faith) and an action to commit (active trust). The development and deepening of the relationship occurs through a repeating process. It is a process in which we have the opportunity to take these three steps with layer after layer of our being. Our deepest beliefs are tested in the fires of life and we decide either to be available to learn the lessons that He desires to teach us or we decide to be unavailable.

God has encouraged us to learn about Him through his word. We see in Romans that the result of that learning can be faith if we choose to accept the new ideas.

Faith comes by hearing … Romans 10:17.

Remember, we defined faith as allowing ourselves to have hope in an idea. Jesus taught us about the importance of allowing ourselves to believe. In the parable of the sower and the seed (Luke 8) He teaches that the condition of the heart determines the extent that the word can take root. The person's heart must be the good ground that is not shallow in its commitment nor rocky with concerns for other things. If it is good ground then the result will be faith in the word. If a person has faith (a hope in something unseen) then he or she is in a position to take steps in active trust based upon that faith. In taking active steps in the real world the concept (or relationship) is tested and proven in our hearts to be true experientially.

The assimilation process for our relationship with God as laid out above can be a lot to digest. Let's take each step one at a time.

Recognize the Concept - Realm of the Mind

God has told us clearly from his word that it is His will to work in our lives. His purpose is for good and the ultimate goal is to conform us to the image of His son Jesus Christ. This might sound very obvious to you if you have been involved with Christianity for any length of time. The difficulty is that we don't always live by what is true or what might seem to be obvious. In the recesses of the performance priority belief system even the idea that God has good intentions is suspect. The thought that He actually has a purpose with goals in mind is even more remote. God having a good and wonderful plan that is designed for us personally seems to be, at best, a nice thought that is heard in church once in a while. The inner thought that determines behavior is something like the following: "That's fine for some people but my life doesn't seem to work that way." Fully convinced in the conventional wisdom that "If it is to be, it's up to me," we charge off into our lives assuming that we are solely in control. The result, as we have seen, can be shipwrecked lives. Again, we have to challenge irrational thinking and replace it with the truth. There are a number of references to spiritual growth in God's word that will point us in the right direction.

First, we have to remind ourselves that one of God's functions as disclosed to us in the Bible is to work in us. This is clearly stated in Philippians.

For it is God who is at work in you, both to will and to work for His good pleasure. Philippians 2:13

We also see from Isaiah that one of God's roles is to be our counselor.

...His name will be called Wonderful Counselor, Mighty God, Eternal Father, Prince of Peace. Isaiah 9:6

In Psalms and again in Romans we see that for God's people there is to be an interactive relationship with Him by His Spirit.

For Thou are my Rock and my fortress; for Thy name's sake, Thou will lead me and guide me. Psalms 31: 3

I will instruct you and teach you in the way which you should go; I will counsel you with My eye upon you. Psalms 32:8

For all who are being led by the Spirit of God, these are the sons of God. Romans 8:14

These verses don't speak of a passive set of ideas to live by. What is being said is that there is a living God who relates directly to each of His children.

Next, it is important to remind ourselves of God's essential goodness. The performance belief system is prone to a major error here. When personal efforts do not bring about the expected result the tendency is to believe the worst. The thought might be that I have done all that I can do and God still won't fix this. That must mean that He really isn't a good God. Keep in mind that we don't entertain these thoughts in the forefront of our conscious minds. These are inner beliefs that we acquire along the way as we apply our particular inner priorities to real experiences. Most of us wouldn't dare play that thought intentionally in our minds. The inner belief is there nonetheless and it has a powerful role in how we behave toward God. There are many good scriptures that can be used to counteract this faulty belief. These are some of my favorites:

And those who know Thy name will put their trust in Thee; for thou, O Lord, hast not forsaken those who seek Thee. Psalm 9: 10

The steps of a man are established by the Lord; and He delights in his way. When he falls, he shall not be hurled headlong; because the Lord is the One who holds his hand. Psalms 37: 23.

I will cry to God Most High, to God who accomplishes all things for me. Psalms 57: 2

Bless our God, O peoples, and sound His praise abroad, Who Keeps us in life, and does not allow our feet to slip. Psalms 66: 8-9

I will sing of the lovingkindness of the Lord forever; to all generations I will make known Thy faithfulness with my mouth. Psalms 89: 1

The Lord will accomplish what concerns me ... Psalms 138: 8

For God so loved the world that He gave His only begotten Son, that whoever believes in Him shall not perish, but have eternal life. John 3: 16

For I am convinced that neither death, nor life, nor angels nor principalities, nor things present, nor things to come, nor powers, nor height, nor depth, nor any other created thing, will be able to separate us from the love of God, which is in Christ Jesus our Lord. Romans 8: 38-39

The Lord is my shepherd, I shall not want ...Surely goodness and lovingkindness will follow me all the days of my life. Psalms 23

I am the good shepherd ... John 10:11

Knowing that the first step in the assimilation process is learning then we must be continually exposing ourselves to the truth. The Christian disciplines of reading God's word and listening to solid teaching are good ways to ensure that we are being appropriately exposed.

It is important to note at this point that it is not the Christian disciplines that cause the growth. Some people think that if they just add more discipline they will ensure that they will become spiritual giants. Some like memorization, attending countless meetings, giving in a certain prescribed fashion or volunteering for committees. This behavior is oriented around things to do and is strongly associated with performance oriented thinking, not grace oriented thinking. Unfortunately, those who have become comfortable with these methods of feeling spiritual, generally try to superimpose their beliefs on others. Disciplines and works can all be good in their proper place but they are not responsible for spiritual growth. All that these things do is make us available to the One who is in charge of the process. We cannot hurry His timetable.

On the other side of this thought is the idea that we can delay things that He would like to give us. If we conduct our lives in such a way as to make ourselves unavailable to Him then the gift goes unopened. The proper perspective on doing Christian sounding things is to follow what God has placed in our hearts knowing that our actions in life either make us available to the work of His Spirit or make us unavailable. If we are available when His Spirit moves, then we can take the gift that He has for us. Our hearts can become more closely aligned with the image of who He wants us to be. The gift is His to give. We cannot create it ourselves by performing works. We are only stewards of the lives that he has given us. As good stewards, we are to abstain from sinful practices (things that make us unavailable) and keep the doors of our minds and hearts open to His truth (make ourselves available).

To summarize, the first step in spiritual growth and healing is concerned with the mind and learning. This is a continuous process of exposing ourselves to God's truth and choosing to be available intellectually to the direction of His Spirit.

Embrace a Concept - Realm of the Heart and Spirit

The act of embracing a concept is the next step in the process of spiritual growth and healing. As discussed earlier, the act of choosing to accept a concept is an inner behavior. It engages the heart and can lead to spiritual growth. For our purposes, we will consider the heart to be that part of us that connects us with our spirit. The heart is the very fabric of who we are.

As a man believes in his heart, so he is. Proverbs 23: 7

God, as spirit, lives in our hearts and speaks to us there. Our heart is the part of us that more closely defines who we are as opposed to merely what we understand. It is for that reason that we are more vigilant to protect and guard our hearts. What has become recorded there has allowed us to survive in life to the present point in time. Making waves in this area is much more serious business. The person with a performance priority is the one who survives in life by his or her performance. To allow heart-level changes is to put our very survival on the line. The prospect of change says, "Surprise! Who you are in the present is inadequate for survival!"

That's why we may want to run in the other direction when God begins to speak at the heart level. When He puts His finger on a specific aspect of our survival plan, we might be shaken to the core of our being. Since this is such a fundamental level of change, we are threatened at the lowest levels of who we are. Our natural response is to think that change at this level is too difficult. We have gotten along this

Page 93

far in life with our hearts in the current condition, maybe we can apply what is there more diligently or more often in the hope that the results will turn out to be different somehow. This is where we run into the popular definition of insanity. That definition says that insanity is doing the same thing over and over expecting a different result. When we avoid the truth and apply faulty concepts out of fear, it appears to be insane behavior. Actually, we are just applying what is already recorded in our hearts out of simple desperation.

To get past this step we must allow ourselves to have a hope in something unseen. The phrase "allow ourselves" is important because it is my opinion that all faith is a gift from God. We cannot grit our teeth harder or click our heels together like Dorothy in the Wizard of Oz in order to make something happen. We simply make ourselves available at the level of our hearts. When we make ourselves available in this way, with openness of heart, we can then receive the gift of faith. With the energy of that faith, we make a choice to embrace a concept that we know to be true intellectually. We open our hearts to a concept to make it a part of who we are. At this point we actively change the messages that are playing in our minds. We have already accepted a concept to be true intellectually. Now we must play the concept in our minds through an act of our will and allow it to permeate our heart.

The person with a performance priority might find it difficult to give up the chairperson role on the six committees that they run at the church. They know that so much time taken from their family is destructive to the most critical human relationships that they have. Just as the addict can't let go of his or her substance of choice, the person with a performance priority can't let go of his or her production-based behavior. The powerful belief from the inner survival system says that this is the way to prove self-worth to the Lord. This is the way that I have always earned my position and I certainly can't afford to stop doing this in the area of my relationship to God.

As afflicted people, we must allow ourselves to accept the truth that we know at the level of our mind.

For by grace you have been saved by faith, and that not of yourselves; it is the gift of God, not of works, lest anyone should boast. Ephesians 2: 8

Every fiber of our being tells us that giving up three of the six chairperson positions will cost us our salvation. This is not a new phenomenon. Paul expressed his frustrations with the idea of being justified by works in his letter to the Galatians:

Are you so foolish? Having begun by the Spirit, are you now being perfected by the flesh? Galatians 3: 3

We are likely to feel a significant level of anxiety and fear when our hearts are challenged. In face of the fear we must choose to play the new message of truth. We can make the observation that we are upset and that our feelings don't match up with the new truth, but by faith (hope in something unseen) we choose to embrace that truth. The new message says that we don't have to run every committee at the church to ensure our salvation. The new message says that we must balance our lives and be good stewards of our family relationships as well. As it is allowed to play, the new message begins to have an impact on the anxiety and fear that had taken up residency in our heart. Gradually new emotional reactions are experienced. We discover that allowing the new truth to reside in our hearts makes a difference experientially in our emotional state. Where once there was fear and anxiety regarding an issue in life, peace and love have taken their place.

Take Action on a Concept

It is truly wonderful when spiritual growth results in positive changes in our emotional reactions to life's challenges. It is even more wonderful when that growth evidences itself in new behavior. When new and victorious behavior is shown in situations that were once crippling, we see dramatic proof of real change. Christians, like no other group of people, can say with bubbly enthusiasm, "If you don't like me today, hang around a while. I'm a work in progress"!

This is probably the most exciting part of the three-step process of spiritual growth that we have defined. It is also the most difficult. It is one thing to entertain new thoughts and see new changes in your emotional reactions. It is quite another to actually behave differently. When we see that we must behave differently it becomes painfully obvious that the stakes have been raised on us. If we actually have to do something differently we are betting our actual lives on the new concept or relationship. The inner thought is that if it fails at this level, a piece of us will be lost in the battle. The truth is that, when it succeeds, a new piece is added to our hearts adding strength to who we are.

The person who has been running six committees at church might have a level of peace from choosing to embrace the truth from God's word about freedom. Even so, real release from bondage might not be realized until "one foot is placed in front of the other" in decisive action. The person may not feel like letting go of those committee responsibilities. With knowledge of the appropriate changes to make (step 1) and a new level of peace in his or her heart (step 2) what remains is doing something about it. When this kind of action is taken a real investment of self is made in the new concept or relationship. Everything is being bet on the idea that has been accepted as true. By dramatic action the person is giving God the opportunity to prove Himself to be faithful. As the person lives and moves in the experience of the new truth, it is discovered that the truth can be assimilated at the lowest level.

What If It's Too Hard?

You have probably heard it said many times that the Christian life is full of peaks and valleys. The peaks are those mountaintop experiences when everything is going right. Peace and joy are abundant and life is good. The valleys are those times when life is difficult. Everything is an uphill battle. Sorrow and pain are predominant. We all want to live on the mountaintop. No one likes the painful valley experiences. You may have also heard it said that the fruit in life (spiritual change) is not grown on the mountaintops. It is grown in the valleys. The Bible directly addresses the fact that we will have difficulties in life. It explains what they are for and what our proper response should be.

Consider it all joy, my brethren, when you encounter various trials; knowing that the testing of your faith produces endurance. James 1: 2-3

It's difficult to understand why the storms of life come our way. The book of Job paints a vivid picture of the questioning and doubt that can plague us during our trials. Our goal is to be like Job in the end. He passed through his difficulties and stayed faithful to his Creator. In doing so, he gave God the opportunity to prove himself to be faithful.

David was certainly a man that was acquainted with sorrows. The writings about his life and the Psalms that he wrote are testimonies to a two-way relationship based upon faith and trust.

For Thou hast rescued my soul from death, my eyes from tears, my feet from stumbling. I shall walk before the Lord in the land of the living. I believed when I said, "I am greatly afflicted." Psalms 116 8-10

The apostle Peter addressed this issue as well.

Beloved, do not be surprised at the fiery ordeal among you, which comes upon you for your testing, as though some strange thing were happening to you; but to the degree that you share the sufferings of Christ, keep on rejoicing; so that also at the revelation of His glory, you may rejoice with exultation. 1 Peter 4: 12-13

Therefore, let those also who suffer according to the will of God entrust their souls to a faithful Creator in doing what is right. 1 Peter 4: 19

Some have said the there is no real growth apart from suffering. I'm not sure that no growth takes place on the mountaintops, but it seems clear from the Bible that a considerable amount takes place in the valleys. It is always our choice either to make ourselves available to God or to make ourselves unavailable. He leads and we are to follow. If He leads us to a place of difficulty, we have the choice to follow Him or to devise another path of our own making. It always comes down to the decision to choose the relationship with Him over all else.

Hollywood recently turned out a movie that contained some socially redeeming qualities. It is not often that they do, so it is important to provide some positive reinforcement in the form of support. The movie entitled "The Family Man" was billed as a story similar to the classic "It's a Wonderful Life" with Jimmy Stewart. In this story, Nicolas Cage plays a man caught up in a successful business career. He seemed to have every material thing he could possibly desire, but his life was devoid of any meaningful relationships. In a dream, he is confronted with a life that he could have had if he had stayed with the girlfriend of his youth. As the dream unfolds, life continually presents this couple with the worldly temptations of an extravagant lifestyle, career and riches. Each time the couple goes through some grueling and personally painful choices. In the end, they make the choice in favor of their relationship. On three separate instances the following phrase is used, "I choose us!"

Spiritual growth is a process in which we are presented with similar grueling circumstances and we are given a chance to choose. The Holy Spirit leads us, orchestrating the precise situation needed to reach the deficits in the recesses of our hearts. The challenge is to always say to Jesus, "I choose us!"

What has been outlined so far is a process of learning, embracing and behaving that results in spiritual growth. Spiritual growth is actually the development of faith and trust in God. It is not a self-directed process that we can "pump up" in order to become spiritual super-powers. It is a process that is directed and orchestrated by God according to His timetable. He is our Wonderful Counselor. In His wisdom, He determines how fast we move along and what the lessons are to be. Our role in the process is to be a good steward of our lives. In so doing we make ourselves available intellectually, in our hearts and finally in our actions.

Chapter 9
The Experience of Spiritual Change

At this point you might be wondering what this growth experience looks like in real life. It may be difficult to grasp the idea that God would actually play an active role in your personal life. Does He actually design situations that are just for us and then interact with us providing truth and direction? It's one thing to see it in the life of Job or David as portrayed in the Bible but this is now and that was then.

When we think of God's divine leadership we think of the dramatic examples found in the Bible. We remember the stories of the pillar of fire by night and the cloud by day that led the Hebrew nation through the wilderness. Of course, there is the example of the handwriting that miraculously appeared on the wall. There is also Paul's encounter with God on the Damascus road. There were flashes of light along with the sound of a loud voice as Paul was knocked to the ground and blinded.

While God can still move in these ways to get our attention, it is probably more common to see God's leadership exerted in the hearts of his people. Since the heart is the closest link to our spirit, this is where He will work most often. He will speak to us via a subtle nudging in our spirit that lets us know how He feels. The Bible supports the idea that God indeed speaks to His people and that they really hear Him.

My sheep know My voice, and I know them, and they follow me … John 10: 27

There are ways that God can reveal His hand in our lives if we are open to see them. There are times when circumstances fall together so perfectly that the odds against the experience being a random occurrence are staggering. Some people call this phenomenon divine coincidence. It is easy to dismiss these occurrences out of pessimism or to miss them because we are not looking.

Another way He moves is to provide a special level of insight from His word or an inspiration by His Spirit. This is an "Ah ha!" sort of revelation as the Holy Spirit quickens your heart to the truth. This kind of experience is described by two of Jesus followers as they encountered the resurrected Christ on their journey to Emmaus.

Were not our hearts burning within us while He was speaking to us on the road, while He was explaining the Scriptures to us? Luke 24: 32

He will use various sources like the Bible, others in the body of Christ or Christian teaching and preaching. In all cases, it is a good idea to use caution in taking spiritual direction. The Lord has encouraged us to be careful.

Behold I send you out as sheep in the midst of wolves; therefore, be shrewd as serpents, and innocent as doves. Matthew 10: 16

We must use spiritual discernment in all things, especially for sources of spiritual direction. One good approach to appraising things spiritually is to ask the following questions:

1.   What is the reaction of your own heart? What is your personal and inward witness?

2.   What is the reaction of the Body of Christ? Is there a generally negative or positive reaction from others in the church? Use reputable sources for confirmation. If you are in a solid church body go to your pastor or elders.

3.   What is taught in the Bible? What is the scriptural application for this issue? Your search for truth should be in the context of the whole Bible not just a single passage.

4.   What is the general effect? Does it lift up Jesus Christ? Does it promote joy and freedom in Him or does it lead to a feeling of bondage?

God will use more dramatic forms of communication from time to time. I believe in the gift of prophecy and knowledge that sometimes comes directly by His Spirit. I'm not sure that it's His plan for us to come to depend upon miraculous events as everyday occurrences. Most of us don't get postcards from God. Learning to "hear His voice" is a major component in the process of spiritual growth. If we commit ourselves, the Good Shepard will teach us all that we need to know.

Chapter 10
Summary

Many of us have a strong orientation or priority for personal performance as opposed to an acceptance of God's grace by faith. We have learned from painful life experiences that personal performance is critical to our emotional survival. This priority for performance is something that arises very early in life as a part of our personal growth and development. Initially it is a coping mechanism and is used as a compensation for deficits experienced in the areas of affection and personal affirmation. As we enter adulthood this priority in our personality becomes a liability causing difficulty in almost every area of life.

There are a number of things that can be done to alleviate the pain that goes along with this condition. Living a healthy lifestyle, stress reduction and challenging irrational thinking can all reduce the misery. These are interventions at the level of our mind and body. Going further, supernatural change at the level of our heart and subsequently our spirit, can take place as well. At this level we have the least amount of personal control. Since we can't direct its path, change at this level can be the most uncomfortable. It can also result in the most broad-reaching personal transformation. This is where God, by His Holy Spirit, makes changes that result in spiritual growth and healing.   Intervention at this level goes beyond the alleviation of pain. This kind of change actually reworks the dysfunctional developmental connections that were made in our youth. Our hearts are actually remade in an image of wholeness (image of Christ) as opposed to brokenness.

It is in that image of wholeness that we can reenter the challenging situations of life with new strength. Not only are the challenges of life less painful than before but, in this new strength, we experience victory over circumstances that were previously impossible.

There is a potential for positive change when we are open to the prospect of it all. When we make ourselves available to the truth by learning, accepting and moving ahead in active trust, healing and growth can take place. When we witness actual change in this way, we are seeing the miracle of authentic transformation occurring in our own hearts. That miracle enables us to avoid the complications that arise when we try to make our way through life in our own strength. It is when we transcend and rise above that maze of complications, that we are able to walk fully into the plan that God has made for us. The end result is that we look and act more like the person God created us to be. That kind of authenticity is true freedom, joy and happiness. That is my prayer for you.

References

Bourne, E. (1997). <u>The Anxiety & Phobia Workbook</u>. Oakland, California: New Harbinger Publications.

Childre, D (1998). <u>Freeze Frame</u>. Boulder Creek, California: Planetary Publications.

Cloud, H., Townsend, J. (1992). <u>Boundaries</u>. Grand Rapids, Michigan: Zondervan Publishing House.

Corey, G. (1996). <u>Theory and Practice of Counseling and Psychotherapy.</u> Pacific Grove, California: Brooks / Cole.

Forman, J., Myers D. (1987) <u>The Personal Stress Reduction Program.</u> Englewood Cliffs, New Jersey: Prentice-Hall.

Johnson, D., VanVonderen, J. (1991). <u>The Subtle Power of Spiritual Abuse</u>. Minneapolis, Minnesota: Bethany House.

Matheny, K., Riordan, R. (1992). <u>Stress and Strategies for Lifestyle Management.</u> Atlanta, Georgia: Georgia State University Business Press.

McDonald, A. (Speaker). (2001). <u>Early Memories and the Stages of Development in Psychotherapy</u> AACC Convention. Nashville, Tennessee.

McMinn, M. (1996). <u>Psychology, Theology, and Spirituality in Christian Counseling</u>. Wheaton, Illinois: Tyndale House Publishers.

Olsen, D. (1998). <u>Prepare / Enrich.</u> Minneapolis, Minnesota: Life Innovations.

Propst, L. (1988). <u>Psychotherapy in a Religious Framework</u>. New York: Human Sciences Press.

Schulenburg, N. (2002). <u>Memoirs from the Rear Pew</u>. Enumclaw, Washington: Wine Press.

Seligman, M.E.P. (1974). Depression and learned helplessness. In. Davison & Neale, *Abnormal Psychology.* New York: John Wiley & Sons.

Shapiro, F (2001). Eye Movement Desensitization and Reprocessing. New York: Guilford Press.

Thomas, R. (1996). Comparing Theories of Child Development. Pacific Grove, California: Brooks/Cole

Vanvonderen, J. (1989). Tired of Trying to Measure Up. Minneapolis, Minnesota: Bethany House.

VanVonderen, J. (1995). When God's People Let You Down. Minneapolis, Minnesota: Bethany House

About the Author

Dr. Schulenburg lives in the Golden Isles coastal region of South Georgia. By profession he is a psychotherapist practicing in the area of trauma recovery. His specialty area is memory resolution. He is an active proponent of Adaptive Information Processing Theory and Cognitive Behavioral Theory.

Dr. Schulenburg has written several books and articles. Many of his works explain how theological principles integrate with what is known and verified by research in the field of psychology. His article addressing neurological conditions was published by the Journal of Neurotherapy in 1999. He is a board certified Professional Counselor and a certified EMDR (Eye Movement Desensitization and Reprocessing) Therapist.

He completed his graduate education with the following academic institutions focusing on clinical mental health.
Georgia State University / Psychological Studies Institute MS Professional Counseling
Logos Christian College and Graduate School Ph.D. Psychology